Southern
Electrics

A View From The Past

GRAHAM WATERER

Ian Allan
PUBLISHING

Front cover, top: MTB No S10719S of 2HAL unit
No 2601 stands in Eastleigh yard.
Colour-Rail/B. J. Swain

Front cover, bottom left: An LSWR era poster.
G. Waterer Collection

Front cover, bottom right: Southern Railway poster
dating from 1939. *G. Waterer Collection*

Back cover, top: 4COR No 3153 heads the
12.50pm Waterloo-Portsmouth Harbour service
through Vauxhall on 21 June 1960. *J. Scrace*

Back cover, centre: Approaching London Bridge
4DD Nos 4002/1 form a Gravesend-Charing Cross
service on 29 April 1954. *R. C. Riley*

Back cover, bottom: Southern Railway poster
dating from 1937. *G. Waterer Collection*

Title page:
The 'Belle' passing Copyhold Junction on a
London-bound service, 5BEL No 3052 leading,
on 3 July 1951. *Ian Allan Library*

First published 1998

ISBN 0 7110 2621 1

© Ian Allan Publishing Ltd 1998

Published by Ian Allan Publishing

an imprint of Ian Allan Publishing Ltd,
Terminal House, Station Approach, Shepperton
Surrey TW17 8AS.
Printed by Ian Allan Printing Ltd,
Riverdene Business Park, Molesey Road,
Hersham, Surrey KT12 4RG.

Code: 9810/B

Contents

Introduction   4

History and Rolling Stock   5

Southern Electric Route Headcodes   10

Electric Stock in Use Between 1909 and 1962   14

Route Indicators for Electric Trains   42

Overnight Berthing Allocations of Electric Stock to Depots
and Stations, Summer 1955   77

Left:
An early view of Brighton
Belle all-Pullman unit
No 3052, seen here at
Brighton without roof boards;
at this time it ran as the
'Southern Belle' and was
numbered 2052.
Ian Allan Library

Right:
The compartments of the 4101
type proved to have too little
knee space between seat
benches, so the next design
allowed 6ft between partition
centres, a dimension which
was honoured for the next 45
years, until the designers of
the Networker range decided
that as passengers were getting
bigger, they should be given
less space to sit in. This view
shows a compartment of unit
No 4111, complete with
passengers typical of the
period: Homburg hat, belted
raincoat and cigarette.
Ian Allan Library

Introduction

This book is a pictorial recollection of the Southern electric system, from the start of electrification by the Southern Railway's predecessors, through the Southern Railway and early Southern Region years to 1962, when the second part of the Kent coast electrification was completed — some 50 years of what we might call the Herbert Walker vision. Any kind of railway rolling stock and operation has always fascinated me, especially Southern electrics from my earliest days as the first house I lived in was beside the line near Lordship Lane station on the now closed Nunhead to Crystal Palace (High Level) branch.

The branch had a 20min service from Blackfriars to Crystal Palace on weekdays. It had been closed during World War 2 and used for storing wagons and, it is said, carriages, including the buffet cars of the Mid-Sussex line's 4BUF units. Before and after World War 2, it was worked with three-car units — singly in the off-peak, and as six-car trains in the peak hours. When reopened after the war, it was worked as a shuttle from Nunhead, with just one three-car unit, losing its Sunday service in September 1948. I remember unit No 1289, of the 1925 Guildford / Dorking batch, still in dark green and lined out. Then there were some two-car NOL units — Nos 1849, 1878 and others — far from their South Coast and Windsor homes. Then the three-car

units were augmented to 4SUB, the NOLs returned to their former duties, and a single unit sufficed for the branch.

Then came a family move to Clapham Junction. The railway scene could hardly have been more different. Instead of single SUB units there were all varieties of main-line electrics, from pairs of NOLs to 12-car coastal expresses; it was possible to see every Southern electric unit without going anywhere else, although admittedly it could take a long time to see all the HAL units. There was plenty of steam then and it still dominated some lines, but I maintained that electrics were the best, with few experiences to beat hammering down the Portsmouth line in a 4COR motor coach.

There have been many changes since those years; the friendly green paint has gone and there are no dimly lit route headcodes at night; now there is yellow paint and a dazzling headlight on every front end, and in the future there will be no slam door carriages as they must have sliding doors. But the past can still be with us; a few of us recorded it with our cameras and notebooks. I should like to thank Ian Allan for their help and access to their library of photographs, and also Laurie Mack, for his help and loan of photographs; without them, this collection could not have been produced.

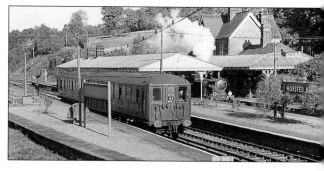

Right:
A BIL on the 'Bluebell' at Horstead Keynes on 27 October 1962. Electric services to Haywards Heath finished on 18 October 1963. The sidings in the foreground were removed, but have now been reinstated. In the background, E4 No 473 is working the 2.20pm to Sheffield Park, whilst 2BIL No 2115 is about to leave for Seaford.
Ian Allan Library

History and Rolling Stock

A few words are needed to explain the occasional references to the constituent parts of the Southern Railway and Southern Region over the half century covered by this collection. The areas and character of the London and South Western Railway (L&SWR), South Eastern & Chatham Railway (SE&CR) and London Brighton & South Coast Railway (LB&SCR) have changed little, even in recent years. The organisation of the Southern Railway and of British Railways Southern Region — and after them, the privately owned South West Trains, Connex South Central and Connex South Eastern — have persistently followed the company geography of a century ago.

A year or two after the Grouping in 1923, the L&SWR area became the Western Section of the Southern Railway, and under BR it became the South Western Division. Similarly, the SE&CR area became the Eastern Section, then the South Eastern Division. The LB&SCR, after a brief spell as the Brighton Section, became the Central Section, then the Central Division. In addition, for some purposes, there were London West, London Central, London East, Southern (which was actually centred on Hampshire and Dorset) and Western (Devon and Cornwall). Not surprisingly, the operating areas came to be known familiarly as Western, Central and Eastern, so that the precise meaning of 'South London' often had to be worked out from its context. The Central Section also gave its name to the Southern's standard multiple-unit brake gear.

Rolling stock descriptions have been similarly tenacious over the years, despite the imposition of computer codes in the 1970s. The telegraphic codes such as 2BIL, 4COR, 4SUB were actually quite late on the scene — it was not until 1933 that electric multiple-units were given them — but they stuck, and even if it is 'Class 411' in the

1998 carriage working notices, a 4CEP is still 'CEP' to many people (note that, strictly speaking, it is 'Cep' and not, as it is usually printed, 'CEP' with capital letters). The term 4SUB appears to date from 1941, when the first four-car suburban units appeared, needing their own code.

The Southern Railway / Southern Region multiple-unit type codes referred to in this book indicate the general type and formation of the motor units for operating purposes and do not distinguish between sub-types. They are listed below, in unit number series order, with the period in which most of them ran. The word 'car' is used here (eg, two-car unit); the Southern used 'car' or 'coach' interchangeably; the unit codes could be printed with a hyphen, or without. All units were motored; by convention, an unmotored formation was a 'set'.

2	two-car trailer set, various sub-types, series 989-1200 (1920-48)
3	three-car suburban unit, various sub-types, series 1201-800 (1914-49)
2SL	two-car South London line units, 1801 type (1929-54)
2WIM	two-car Wimbledon-West Croydon line units, 1809 type (1929-54)
2NOL	two-car non-lavatory units, 1813 type (1934-36 / 1957-59)
2BIL	two-car lavatory units, 2001 type, lavatory in both coaches (1935-39 / 1969-71)
2HAL	two-car lavatory units, 2601 type, lavatory in one coach (1939-48 / 1969-71)
4LAV	four-car units with one lavatory coach, 2921 type (1932-68)
6PUL	six-car unit with Pullman car, 3001 type (originally 2001 etc, coded 6COR) (1933-66)

6PAN   six-car unit with pantry car, 3021 type (originally 2021-37) (1935-66)

6CIT   six-coach unit with Pullman car, 3041 type (originally 2041 etc, coded 6COR) (1933-66)

5BEL   five-coach all-Pullman unit, 3051 type (originally 2051 etc, coded 5PUL) (1933-73)

4RES   four-coach unit with restaurant facilities, 3054 type (1937-**)

4GRI   3054 type with kitchen car altered to griddle car *circa* 1961-2** (3086 type)

4BUF   four-coach unit with buffet car, 3073 type (1938-71)

4COR   four-coach unit, corridor throughout, 3101 type (1938-71)

4DD   four-coach double-deck unit, numbers 4001/2 (later 4901/2)

4SUB   four-car suburban unit, various sub-types, numbers in series 4101-754 (1941-81)

4EPB   four-car suburban unit with electro-pneumatic brake and 'buckeye' couplings, numbers originally in series 5001-370 (1951-95)

2EPB   two-car suburban unit with electro-pneumatic brake and 'buckeye' couplings, numbers originally 5651-84, 5701-95, 5800 (1954-95)

2HAP   two-car lavatory unit with electro-pneumatic brake and 'buckeye' couplings, numbers originally 5601-36, 6001-173 (1957-92)

4CEP   four-car corridor unit, numbers originally 7101-211 (from 1956)

4BEP   four-car corridor unit with buffet car, numbers originally 7001-22 (from 1956)

MLV   one-car motor luggage van (car numbers 68001-10; no unit numbers)

**Some 4RES units were altered; three kitchen cars became griddle cars for the 4GRI units; other kitchen cars were withdrawn and replaced by trailer seconds (4COR [N]) or by Pullman cars from 6PUL units (4PUL). All COR and RES units were withdrawn by 1971.

Right:
When the Southern Railway was formed on 1 January 1923, it inherited two substantial electrified systems: from the London & South Western Railway, a 600V direct current third rail system; and from the London Brighton & South Coast Railway, a single phase alternating current overhead wire system at 6,700V, 25 cycles. There was also the Waterloo & City Line, which had been promoted by the L&SWR, opened in 1898, and absorbed in 1907; but it never seemed to catch the imagination as part of the Southern Electric system.

   The LB&SCR decided to electrify its suburban area, starting with the South London Line (Victoria-Peckham Rye-London Bridge) on which public services commenced on 1 December 1909. This was followed by Victoria-Crystal Palace-Norwood Junction on 12 May 1911. Because of World War 1, further work had to be deferred and it was not until the Southern Railway was in being that the extension to Coulsdon North and Sutton via Selhurst was completed, on 1 April 1925. The system used was single-phase ac with overhead wires, at 6700V, 25 cycles. The last ac train ran on 22 September 1929. Seen here on the South London line in March 1928 is a two-coach set on a London Bridge-Victoria service at Denmark Hill.
H. C. Casserley

Below right:
South London line ac two-coach set at Peckham Rye in March 1927, still carrying LB&SCR carriage numbers 3204 (motor third brake) and 4057 (driving trailer). No 3204 was given SR number 8603 about 1927 and in April 1929 was converted to dc driving trailer No 9758 in unit No 1808. No 4057 became No 9817 in August 1927; its body was rebuilt as dc motor third brake No 8706 in June 1929, and survived in unit No 1737 and then in 4537 until 1956. Peckham Rye depot's ac use ceased in 1929 but it remained in use for dc trains until the early 1960s, mainly as a lifting shop for main-line electric stock. The depot was situated between Peckham Rye and Denmark Hill; the site is now a housing estate.
Ian Allan Library

SOUTHERN–Western Section 180a

For LOCAL TRAINS and INTERMEDIATE STATIONS between WATERLOO and SURBITON and COMPLETE SERVICE between WATERLOO and GUILDFORD, see pages 194 to 201c.

LONDON, GODALMING, HASLEMERE, PETERSFIELD, and PORTSMOUTH

Mondays to Fridays—*Continued*

Down	aft	aft R	aft	aft	aft	aft R	aft	aft	aft	aft	aft	aft R	aft	ngt.	
LONDON (Waterloo)..dep.	8 27	8 5[illegible]	..	8 57	9 27	9 50	..	9 57	1025	1057	1127	11 50	1150	12 7	..
Surbiton	8 43	..	..	9 13	9 43	..	..	1013	1043	1113	1146	..	..	1223	..
Esher, for Sandown Park	8 47	..	..	9 17	9 47	..	..	1017	1047	1117	1150	..	..	1227	..
Hersham	8 50	..	..	9 20	9 50	..	..	1020	1050	1120	1153	..	..	1230	..
Walton-on-Thames	8 53	..	..	9 23	9 53	..	..	1023	1053	1123	1156	..	..	1233	..
Weybridge A	8 57	..	..	9 27	9 57	..	..	1027	1057	1127	12 0	12 14	1214	1237	..
West Weybridge	9 0	..	..	9 30	10 0	..	..	1030	11 0	1130	12 3	..	..	1240	..
Byfleet B	9 3	..	..	9 33	10 3	..	..	1033	11 3	1133	12 6	..	..	1243	..
Woking C	9 8	..	..	9 38	10 8	..	..	1038	11 8	1138	1211	12 22	1222	1248	..
Worplesdon	9 13	..	..	9 43	1013	..	..	1043	1113	1143	1216	..	..	1253	..
Guildford 192, 236, 290, 292 arr.	9 20	9 25	..	9 50	1020	1025	..	1050	1120	1150	1223	12 31	1231	1 0	..
dep.	..	9 26	9 31	10 1	..	1026	1031	1051	1121	..	..	12 32	1235	..	..
Farncombe	..	..	9 36	10 6	..	..	1036	1056	1126	..	..	..	1240	..	..
Godalming	..	..	9 39	10 9	..	..	1039	1059	1129	..	..	..	1243	..	..
Milford	..	..	9 44	1014	..	..	1044	11 4	1134	..	..	..	1248	..	..
Witley, for Chiddingfold	..	..	9 48	1018	..	..	1048	11 8	1138	..	..	..	1252	..	..
Haslemere D	..	9 45	9 56	1026	..	1045	1056	1116	1146	..	..	12 50	1 0	..	..
Liphook	..	..	10 2	1032	..	..	11 2	1122	1152	..	..	..	1 6	..	..
Liss	..	..	10 9	1039	..	..	11 9	1129	1159	..	..	..	1 13	..	..
Petersfield 180d	..	..	1014	1044	..	..	1114	1134	12 4	..	..	..	1 18	..	..
Rowlands Castle	..	..	1026	1056	..	..	1126	1146	1216	..	..	..	..	..	..
Havant 238, 258	..	..	1031	11 1	..	..	1131	1151	1221	..	..	..	1 34	..	..
Bedhampton Halt	..	..	1033	11 3	..	..	1133	1153	..	..	..	..	..	..	..
Fratton 258	..	..	1041	1111	..	1118	1141	12 1	1231	..	..	1 24	1 43	..	..
Portsmouth & Southsea	..	1020	1044	1114	..	1120	1144	12 4	1233	..	..	1 26	1 46	..	..
" Harbour arr.	..	1025	..	..	..	1125	..	..	..	..	..	1THO31	..	..	..
Ryde Pier 181a (By Boat) "	..	..	..	..	..	..	..	..	..	..	..	3THO20	..	..	..

Wed. nights (Thurs. morns.) only.

Saturdays

Down	mrn	mrn	mrn	mrn	mrn	mrn	mrn	mrn R		mrn R	mrn	mrn	mrn R	mrn R	mrn	mrn
LONDON (Waterloo)..dep.	5 27	5 57	6 27	6 50	..	6 57	7 27	7 45	..	7 50	..	7 57	8 15	8 20	..	8 25
Surbiton	5 45	6 15	6 45	On 31st July only.	..	7 15	7 43	..	..	..	..	8 13	..	..	..	8 43
Esher, for Sandown Park	5 49	6 19	6 49		..	7 19	7 47	..	..	..	..	8 17	..	..	..	8 47
Hersham	5 52	6 22	6 52		..	7 22	7 50	..	..	..	..	8 20	..	..	..	8 50
Walton-on-Thames	5 55	6 25	6 55		..	7 25	7 53	..	..	..	..	8 23	..	..	..	8 53
Weybridge A	5 59	6 29	6 59		..	7 29	7 57	..	..	..	..	8 27	..	..	..	8 57
West Weybridge	6 2	6 32	7 2		..	7 32	8 0	..	..	..	..	8 30	..	..	..	9 0
Byfleet B	6 5	6 35	7 5		..	7 35	8 3	..	..	..	..	8 33	..	..	..	9 3
Woking C	6 12	6 42	7 12		..	7 42	8 8	..	..	..	..	8 38	..	..	..	9 8
Worplesdon	6 17	6 47	7 17		..	7 47	8 13	..	..	..	..	8 43	..	..	..	9 13
Guildford 192, 236, 290, 292 arr.	6 23	6 53	7 23		..	7 53	8 20	..	..	8 25	..	8 50	..	8 56	..	9 20
dep.	6 31	7 1	..	..	7 31	8 1	..	..	..	8 26	8 31	..	..	8 58	9 1	..
Farncombe	6 36	7 6	..	..	7 36	8 6	..	..	..	..	8 36	..	..	..	9 6	..
Godalming	6 39	7 9	..	..	7 39	8 9	..	..	..	..	8 39	..	..	..	9 9	..
Milford	6 44	7 14	..	..	7 44	8 14	..	..	..	..	8 44	..	..	..	9 14	..
Witley, for Chiddingfold	6 48	7 18	..	..	7 48	8 18	..	..	..	..	8 48	..	..	..	9 18	..
Haslemere D	6 56	7 26	..	..	7 56	8 26	..	..	..	8 45	8 56	..	..	..	9 26	..
Liphook	7 2	7 32	..	..	8 2	8 32	..	..	..	..	9 2	..	..	..	9 32	..
Liss	7 9	7 39	..	..	8 9	8 39	..	..	..	..	9 9	..	..	..	9 39	..
Petersfield 180d	7 14	7 44	..	..	8 14	8 44	..	..	..	..	9 14	..	..	..	9 44	..
Rowlands Castle	7 26	7 56	..	..	8 26	8 56	..	..	..	..	9 26	..	..	..	9 56	..
Havant 238, 258	7 31	8 1	..	..	8 31	9 1	..	9 7	..	..	9 31	..	..	..	10 1	..
Bedhampton Halt	7 33	8 3	..	..	8 33	9 3	..	..	..	..	9 33	..	..	..	10 3	..
Fratton 258	7 41	8 11	..	..	8 41	9 11	..	..	..	..	9 41	..	..	..	1011	..
Portsmouth & Southsea	7 44	8 14	..	8 20	8 44	9 14	..	..	..	9 20	9 44	..	9 45	9 53	1014	..
" Harbour arr.	..	..	..	8 25	..	..	..	9 20	..	9 25	..	..	9 50	9 57	..	..
Ryde Pier 181a (By Boat) "	..	..	..	9 20	..	..	..	10 0	..	1015	..	..	1045	1045	..	..

Saturdays—*Continued*

Down	mrn R	mrn R	mrn	mrn	mrn R	mrn R	mrn	mrn	mrn R	mrn R	mrn	mrn	mrn R	mrn R	mrn
LONDON (Waterloo)..dep.	8 45	8 50	..	8 57	9 15	9 20	..	9 27	9 45	9 50	..	9 57	1015	1020	..
Surbiton	..	..	..	9 13	..	..	..	9 43	..	..	..	1013	..	..	..
Esher, for Sandown Park	..	..	..	9 17	..	..	..	9 47	..	..	..	1017	..	..	..
Hersham	..	..	..	9 20	..	..	..	9 50	..	..	..	1020	..	..	..
Walton-on-Thames	..	..	..	9 23	..	..	..	9 53	..	..	..	1023	..	..	..
Weybridge A	..	..	..	9 27	..	..	..	9 57	..	..	..	1027	..	..	..
West Weybridge	..	..	..	9 30	..	..	..	10 0	..	..	..	1030	..	..	..
Byfleet B	..	..	..	9 33	..	..	..	10 3	..	..	..	1033	..	..	..
Woking C	..	..	..	9 38	..	..	..	10 8	..	..	..	1038	..	..	..
Worplesdon	..	..	..	9 43	..	..	..	1013	..	..	..	1043	..	..	..
Guildford 192, 236, 290, 292 arr.	..	9 27	..	9 50	..	9 53	..	1020	..	1025	..	1050	..	1055	..
dep.	..	9 28	9 31	..	..	9 57	10 1	..	..	1026	1031	..	..	1057	11 1
Farncombe	..	..	9 36	..	..	..	10 6	..	..	..	1036	..	..	..	11 6
Godalming	..	..	9 39	..	..	..	10 9	..	..	..	1039	..	..	..	11 9
Milford	..	..	9 44	..	..	..	1014	..	..	..	1044	..	..	..	1114
Witley, for Chiddingfold	..	..	9 48	..	..	..	1018	..	..	..	1048	..	..	..	1118
Haslemere D	..	9 47	9 56	..	..	..	1026	..	..	1045	1056	..	..	..	1126
Liphook	..	..	10 2	..	..	..	1032	..	..	..	11 2	..	..	..	1132
Liss	..	..	10 9	..	..	..	1039	..	..	..	11 9	..	..	..	1139
Petersfield 180d	..	..	1014	..	..	..	1044	..	..	..	1114	..	..	..	1144
Rowlands Castle	..	..	1026	..	..	..	1056	..	..	..	1126	..	..	..	1156
Havant 238, 258	10 7	..	1031	..	..	..	11 1	..	11 7	..	1131	..	..	..	12 1
Bedhampton Halt	..	..	1033	..	..	..	11 3	..	..	..	1133	..	..	..	12 3
Fratton 258	..	..	1041	..	..	..	1111	..	..	..	1141	..	..	..	1211
Portsmouth & Southsea	..	1022	1044	..	1047	1051	1114	..	..	1120	1144	..	1145	1151	1214
" Harbour arr.	1020	1027	..	..	1052	1055	..	..	1120	1125	..	..	1150	1156	..
Ryde Pier 181a (By Boat) "	1115	1115	..	..	1145	1145	..	..	1215	1215	..	..	1245	1245	..

Down	mrn	mrn R	mrn R	mrn	mrn	mrn R	mrn R	aft	mrn	mrn R	mrn R	aft	mrn		aft R	aft R	aft
LONDON (Waterloo)..dep.	1027	1045	1050	..	1057	1115	1120	..	1127	1145	1150	..	1157	..	1215	1220	..
Surbiton	1043	..	..	..	1113	..	..	..	1143	..	..	..	1213	..	..	..	..
Esher, for Sandown Park	1047	..	..	..	1117	..	..	..	1147	..	..	..	1217	..	..	..	..
Hersham	1050	..	..	..	1120	..	..	..	1150	..	..	..	1220	..	..	..	..
Walton-on-Thames	1053	..	..	..	1123	..	..	..	1153	..	..	..	1223	..	..	..	..
Weybridge A	1057	..	..	..	1127	..	..	..	1157	..	..	..	1227	..	..	..	..
West Weybridge	11 0	..	..	..	1130	..	..	..	12 0	..	..	..	1230	..	..	..	..
Byfleet B	11 3	..	..	..	1133	..	..	..	12 3	..	..	..	1233	..	..	..	..
Woking C	11 8	..	..	..	1138	..	..	..	12 8	..	..	..	1238	..	..	..	..
Worplesdon	1113	..	..	..	1143	..	..	..	1213	..	..	..	1243	..	..	..	..
Guildford 192, 236, 290, 292 arr.	1120	..	1125	..	1150	..	1155	..	1220	..	1225	..	1250	..	..	1255	..
dep.	..	..	1126	1131	..	..	1156	12 1	..	..	1226	1231	..	..	..	1256	1 1
Farncombe	..	..	..	1136	..	..	..	12 6	..	..	..	1236	..	..	..	..	1 6
Godalming	..	..	..	1139	..	..	..	12 9	..	..	..	1239	..	..	..	1 3	1 9
Milford	..	..	..	1144	..	..	..	1214	..	..	..	1244	..	..	..	..	1 14
Witley, for Chiddingfold	..	..	..	1148	..	..	..	1218	..	..	..	1248	..	..	..	..	1 18
Haslemere D	..	..	1145	1156	..	..	..	1226	..	..	1245	1256	..	..	..	1 15	1 26
Liphook	..	..	..	12 2	..	..	..	1232	..	..	..	1 2	..	..	..	..	1 32
Liss	..	..	..	12 9	..	..	..	1239	..	..	..	1 9	..	..	..	..	1 39
Petersfield 180d	..	..	..	1214	..	..	..	1244	..	..	..	1 14	..	..	..	1c32	1 44
Rowlands Castle	..	..	..	1226	..	..	..	1256	..	..	..	1 26	..	..	..	..	1 56
Havant 238, 258	..	12 7	..	1231	..	..	..	1 1	..	1 7	..	1 31	..	..	..	1 48	2 1
Bedhampton Halt	..	..	..	1233	..	..	..	1 3	..	..	..	1 33	..	..	..	..	2 3
Fratton 258	..	..	..	1241	..	..	..	1 11	..	..	..	1 41	..	..	..	..	2 11
Portsmouth & Southsea	..	..	1220	1244	..	1245	1250	1 14	..	..	1 20	1 44	..	..	1 45	1 59	2 14
" Harbour arr.	..	1220	1225	..	..	1250	1255	..	..	1 20	1 25	..	..	..	1 50	2 3	..
Ryde Pier 181a (By Boat) "	..	1 15	1 15	..	..	1 45	1 45	..	..	2 15	2 15	..	..	..	2 45	2 45	..

For Notes see page 180d.

Southern Railway summer timetable, July 4-September 26 1937

Right:
Eight three-car sets (each with two motor third brakes with a trailer first between) were built by the Metropolitan Amalgamated Carriage & Wagon Co at Birmingham. By 1912 the three-car formations had been altered to two cars by taking out the trailer firsts and coupling a driving trailer composite, converted from steam stock, to each motor brake.

Two two-coach South London ac sets are pictured at Clapham on 17 March 1928. Note the conductor rail in position ready for conversion to dc operation. *Ian Allan Library/ H. C. Casserley*

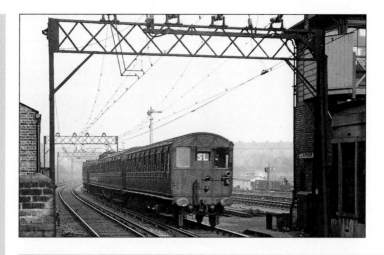

Right:
LB&SCR Crystal Palace stock in Streatham Hill sidings, probably about 1912 when new. *Ian Allan Library/Madgwick Collection*

Below:
South London motor third brake No 3201, built by the Metropolitan Amalgamated Railway Carriage & Wagon Co in 1909. Renumbered by the SR in February 1925 to 8601, it was converted to dc driving trailer composite No 9751 in April 1929. *G. Waterer Collection*

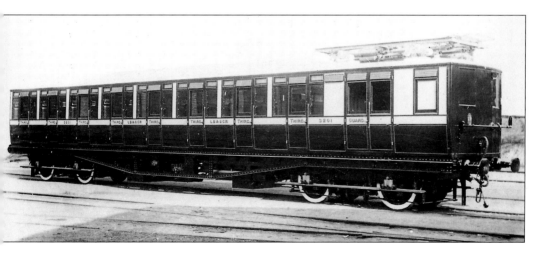

Southern Electric
Route Headcodes

The LB&SCR was the first railway to use numbers as route indicators instead of the disc/lamp system used on steam locomotives, adopting them for its new electric services to Crystal Palace in 1911. Front-end destination boards were also fitted. The L&SWR was not far behind, but used letters instead of numbers when electrics began regular operation in 1915, without destination boards. The term 'headcode' was adopted to describe the system.

The LB&SC arrangement was a painted board on the cab front, lit from above; the South Western was rather more sophisticated, using an iron stencil plate in front of an opal glass panel, lit from inside at night. The South Western letter headcode system was adopted for new dc electric routes, but although the individual letters were modified by a bar above, or in Southern Railway days by dots, it was limited in its scope. For main line services, therefore, numbers were used, and in the late 1930s, for the sake of simplicity, numbers were allocated to all suburban routes. At first these were used only when main line stock ran on suburban duties, but from 1941 all new suburban units were fitted with number plates. No effort was made to rationalise the system, however, and the first-generation suburban units kept their letter plates to the end.

The letter plates used by the L&SWR were H, I, O, P, S and V, leading to the celebrated advert with five trains supposedly side by side showing H O V I S, complete with a bar over the O. The SR added J, L, N, T and U, and inverted P and inverted V. The letter system was really limited by what could be cut as a stencil without the iron plate being weakened, and the need to avoid any letter which could be confused with others. Although C, F and Z might have qualified, the alphabet seems to have been abandoned without giving them a trial.

Except for the '2' plates carried by the South London and Wimbledon-West Croydon units, which were the standard suburban type, all number plates came as a set, 0 to 9, plus a blank, any two of which were slid into a wrought-iron frame held rather insecurely on the heacode box on the cab front by two fixed brackets and one movable one. On empty trains a bar was added above the number. Plates not in use were carried in a rack in the driver's cab, or on 4COR and similar units, in the guard's van.

From the end of 1951, all new stock was fitted with roller blinds; the blinds eventually included a red blank exposure, and from 1965 Eastern section trains ran without oil tail lamps at the rear; the red blind, lit at night, served the purpose better.

Above right:
For the Crystal Palace services, 30 motor third brakes, and 60 driving trailer composites were built in 1911-2 and four more motor third brakes and eight driving trailers were added later; construction was divided between Metropolitan and the LB&SCR's Lancing works. They were known, logically, as the 'Crystal Palace' or 'CP' stock. Crystal Palace motor coach No 3260, built by MRC&W in 1911, is seen here. This was converted in January 1930 to dc trailer No 9281 for set 1180; this lasted until about 1947.
Ian Allan Library/O. J. Morris

Centre right:
Crystal Palace three-coach set as used in the first trial of electro-pneumatic braking in 1927 in Selhurst depot. It was to be nearly 25 years before ep brakes were adopted by the Southern, on its EPB stock of 1951. Note the conductor rail in the foreground. *Ian Allan Library*

Right:
Passing Wandsworth Common on 17 March 1928, a set of Crystal Palace stock bound for Victoria. The background is little changed today.
Ian Allan Library/H. C. Casserley

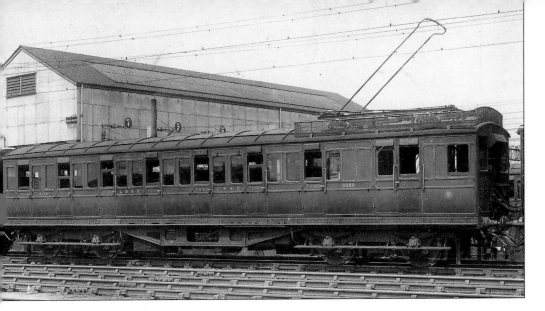

Table 31

LONDON, NEW BECKENHAM, HAYES, ADDISCOMBE (CROYDON), and SANDERSTEAD

Table 31 — 3—All Trains on this page are Third class only

FOR NOTES, SEE PAGE 56

Mls	Down	a.m.—Week Days—a.m.																					
										SX				SX							Saturdays only		
—	Charing Cross ...... dep	..	..	..	5 9	..	5 36	..	6 1	..	..	..	6 38	..	..	6 54	6 58	..	7 15	7 23	..	..	7 36
½	Waterloo	....	....	....	5 11	....	5 38	....	6 3	..	....	....	6 40	....	....	6 56	7 0	....	7 17	7 25	....	....	7 38
—	Cannon Street	..	4 50	..	..	5 30	..	5 48	..	6 11	6 14	6 22	..	6 45	6 46	..	..	7 11	..	..	..	7 34	..
1¾	London Bridge	....	4 55	....	5 17	5 35	5 44	5 51	6 7	6 14	6 18	6 26	6 44	6 48	6 50	7 0	7 5	7 14	7 21	7 29		7 37	7 43
4¼	New Cross	..	5 1	..	5 23	5 40	5 51	5 58	6 13	6 20	6 24	6 33	6 50	6 54	6 57	7 6	7 11	7 20	7 27	7 36		7 43	7 48
5¼	St. John's	....	....	....	5 25	....	5 54	6 0	6 15	..	6 26	....	....	....	7 0	....	....	....	....	..		....	....
6	Lewisham	..	..	..	5 28	..	5 57	6 3	6 17	..	6 28	6 37	6 53	..	7 2	..	..	7 23	..	..		7 46	..
6¾	Lady Well	....	5 6	....	5 30	5 45	5 59	6 5	6 19	6 24	[illegible]	6 39	....	6 58	7 4	....	7 15	..	7 31	7 41		....	7 53
7½	Catford Bridge	..	5 8	..	5 34	5 47	6 1	6 7	6 22	6 27	6 33	6 43	6 56	7 1	7 6	7 13	7 18	7 28	7 34	7 43		7 50	7 55
9	Lower Sydenham	....	5 11	....	5 37	5 50	6 4	6 10	6 25	6 30	6 36	6 46	....	7 4	7 9	7 16	7 21	..	7 37	7 46		7 53	7 58
9½	New Beckenham	..	5 13	..	5 40	5 52	6 6	6 12	6 27	6 32	6 38	6 49	..	7 6	7 11	7 18	7 23	..	7 39	7 48		7 55	..
10¼	Clock House	..	5 16	..	5 42	5 55	6 9	6 15	6 29	6 34	6 40	6 51	7 1	7 8	7 14	7 21	7 25	..	7 41	7 51		7 57	..
11	Elmer's End ...... arr	....	5 18	....	5 44	5 58	6 11	6 17	6 31	6 36	6 42	6 53	7 3	7 10	7 16	7 23	7 27	7 34	7 43	7 53	..	7 59	8 3
	Elmer's End ...... dep	4 44	5 18	5 20	5 44	5 58	6 11	6 17	6 31	6 36	6 42	6 53	7 3	7 10	7 16	7 23	7 27	7 34	7 43	7 53	7 57	7 59	8 3
12¼	Eden Park .... dep	....	....	5 23	....	6 2	....	6 21	....	6 40	6 46	....	7 7	....	7 19	....	7 31	....	7 47	....	..	8 3	....
13½	West Wickham	..	..	5 25	..	6 4	..	6 23	..	6 42	6 50	..	7 9	..	7 22	..	7 33	..	7 49	..	..	8 5	..
14½	Hayes A .... arr	4 50	....	5 29	....	6 8	...	6 27	....	6 46	6 54	....	7 13	....	7 25	....	7 37	....	7 53	....	..	8 9	....
12	Woodside (Surrey)	..	5 20	..	5 47	..	6 13	..	6 35	..	..	6 57	..	7 13	..	7 25	..	7 36	..	7 55	8 0	..	8 5
13	Addiscombe C .... arr	....	5 23	....	5 50	....	....	....	....	..	....	....	....	7 16	....	....	....	7 39	....	....	8 3	....	8 8
12¾	Bingham Road	..	..	..	..	..	6 16	..	6 37	..	..	6 59	..	..	..	7 28	..	..	..	7 57	..	..	..
13¾	Coombe Road	....	....	....	....	....	6 19	....	6 40	..	....	7 2	....	....	....	7 31	....	....	....	8 0	....	....	....
14¼	Selsdon	..	..	..	..	..	6 21	..	6 42	..	..	7 8	..	..	..	7 33	..	..	..	8 2	..	..	..
15	Sanderstead .... arr	....	....	....	....	....	6 23	....	6 44	..	....	7 10	....	....	....	7 35	....	....	....	8 5	....	....	....

Down	a.m.—Week Days—a.m.						a.m.—Mondays to Fridays—a.m.																
Charing Cross ...... dep	7 38	7 48	7 52	7 58	..	..	8 1	..	..	..	..	8 33	..	..	..	8 49	8 58	9 8	..	..	..	..	9 33
Waterloo	7 40	7 50	7 54	8 1	....	....	8 3	..	....	....	....	8 35	..	..	..	8 51	9 0	9 10	..	..	..	....	9 35
Cannon Street	..	..	..	..	..	..	..	8 9	8 14	8 21	8 25	....	8 36	8 45	8 50	..	..	..	9 21	9 25	..	9 30	..
London Bridge	7 46	7 55	7 59	8 6	....	....	8 7	8 12	8 17	8 24	8 29	8 39	8 40	8 48	8 53	8 58	9 5	9 15	9 24	9 29	..	9 35	9 40
New Cross	7 52	8 1	..	..	..	..	8 13	8 18	8 23	8 30	8 35	..	8 47	8 54	8 59	9 3	..	9 20	9 30	9 34	..	9 40	9 46
St. John's	....	....	....	8 12	....	....	8 16	..	..	8 33	....	....	8 49	..	..	....	....	....	..	9 37	..	9 43	..
Lewisham	7 55	8 4	..	8 14	..	..	..	8 21	..	8 35	..	..	8 51	..	9 2	..	..	..	9 33	9 39	..	9 45	..
Lady Well	7 57	....	8 8	..	....	....	....	8 23	8 28	..	8 39	8 48	8 53	8 58	..	9 8	9 14	9 25	9 35	..	..	9 47	9 51
Catford Bridge	8 0	8 7	8 10	8 17	..	..	8 21	8 25	8 30	..	8 42	8 50	8 56	9 1	9 5	9 10	9 16	..	9 37	9 42	..	9 49	9 53
Lower Sydenham	8 3	8 10	8 13	8 20	....	....	....	8 28	8 33	8 40	8 45	8 53	8 59	9 4	9 8	9 13	9 20	9 29	9 40	9 45	..	9 52	9 57
New Beckenham	8 5	8 12	8 16	..	..	..	8 25	8 30	..	8 42	8 47	8 55	..	9 6	9 10	9 15	9 22	9 31	9 42	9 47	..	9 55	9 59
Clock House	8 7	8 14	8 19	8 24	..	..	8 27	..	8 37	8 44	8 49	8 58	9 2	9 8	9 13	9 18	9 24	9 34	9 45	9 50	..	..	10 1
Elmer's End ...... arr	8 9	8 16	8 21	8 26	....	....	8 29	8 34	8 39	8 46	8 52	9 0	9 4	9 11	9 15	9 20	9 26	9 36	9 47	9 52	..	..	10 3
Elmer's End ...... dep	8 9	8 16	8 21	8 26	..	..	8 29	8 34	8 39	8 46	8 52	9 1	9 4	9 11	9 15	9 20	9 26	9 36	9 47	9 52	9 54	..	10 3
Eden Park .... dep	8 13	..	8 24	....	....	....	8 33	....	8 42	8 50	....	..	9 8	9 14	..	....	9 29	9 39	..	9 55	..	....	..
West Wickham	8 15	..	8 27	..	..	..	8 35	..	8 45	8 52	..	..	9 10	9 17	..	..	9 32	9 42	..	9 58	..	..	..
Hayes A .... arr	8 19	..	8 30	....	....	....	8 39	....	8 48	8 56	....	..	9 14	9 20	..	....	9 35	9 45	..	10 1	..	....	..
Woodside (Surrey)	..	8 19	..	8 28	..	..	..	8 36	..	..	8 55	9 3	..	..	9 17	9 22	..	..	9 49	..	9 56	..	10 6
Addiscombe C .... arr	....	....	..	8 31	....	....	....	....	....	....	8 58	....	....	..	..	9 25	....	..	..	....	9 59	..	10 9
Bingham Road	..	8 21	..	..	..	..	..	8 38	..	..	..	9 5	..	..	9 19	..	..	..	9 51	..	..	..	..
Coombe Road	....	8 24	..	....	....	....	....	8 41	....	....	....	9 8	..	....	9 22	..	....	....	9 54	....	..	....	..
Selsdon	..	8 26	..	..	..	..	..	8 44	..	..	..	9 10	..	..	9 24	..	..	..	9 56	..	..	..	..
Sanderstead .... arr	....	....	..	....	....	....	....	8 47	....	....	....	9 13	..	....	9 27	..	....	....	9 59	....	..	....	..

Down	a.m.—Mondays to Fridays—a.m.																					p.m
Charing Cross ...... dep	9 38	..	9 46	..	9 58	10 7	..	..	1022	..	1037	..	1052	..	11 7	..	1122	..	1137	..	1152	..
Waterloo	9 40	..	9 48	..	10 0	10 9	..	..	1024	..	1039	..	1054	..	11 9	....	1124	..	1139	..	1154	..
Cannon Street	..	..	..	10 0	..	..	1016	1020	..	..	..	1050	..	..	..	1120	..	..	..	11 50	..	..
London Bridge	9 45	..	9 52	10 3	10 5	1013	1019	1024	1028	..	1043	1053	1058	..	1113	1123	1128	..	1143	11 53	1158	..
New Cross	9 50	..	9 58	10 9	1011	1019	1025	1029	1034	..	1049	1058	11 4	..	1119	1128	1134	..	1149	11 58	12 4	..
St. John's	9 53	..	10 0	..	1014	1021	1027	1032	1036	..	..	11 1	11 6	..	..	1131	1136	..	..	12 1	12 6	..
Lewisham	9 56	..	10 3	1012	1016	1023	..	1034	..	..	1052	11 3	..	..	1122	1133	..	..	1152	12 3	..	..
Lady Well	9 58	..	10 5	..	1018	1025	1031	1036	1040	..	1054	11 5	1110	..	1124	1135	1140	..	1154	12 5	1210	..
Catford Bridge	10 0	..	10 7	1015	1020	1028	1033	1038	1042	..	1056	11 7	1112	..	1126	1137	1142	..	1156	12 7	1212	..
Lower Sydenham	10 3	..	1010	1018	1023	1031	1036	1041	1045	..	1059	1110	1115	..	1129	1140	1145	..	1159	12 10	1215	..
New Beckenham	10 5	..	1012	1020	1025	1033	1039	1043	1047	..	11 1	1112	1117	..	1131	1142	1147	..	12 1	12 12	1217	..
Clock House	10 8	..	1015	1022	1028	1035	..	1046	1050	..	11 4	1115	1120	..	1134	1145	1150	..	12 4	12 15	1220	..
Elmer's End ...... arr	1010	..	1017	1024	1030	1037	..	1048	1052	..	11 6	1117	1122	..	1136	1147	1152	..	12 6	12 17	1222	..
Elmer's End ...... dep	1010	1012	1017	1024	1030	1037	..	1048	1052	1056	11 6	1117	1122	1126	1136	1147	1152	1156	12 6	12 17	1222	1226
Eden Park .... dep	1013	..	..	1028	..	1041	..	..	1055	..	11 9	..	1125	..	1138	..	1155	..	12 9	..	1225	..
West Wickham	1016	..	..	1030	..	1043	..	..	1058	..	1112	..	1128	..	1142	..	1158	..	1212	..	1228	..
Hayes A .... arr	1019	..	..	1034	..	1047	..	..	11 1	..	1115	..	1131	..	1145	..	12 1	..	1215	..	1231	..
Woodside (Surrey)	..	1014	1019	..	1032	..	..	1050	..	1058	..	1119	..	1128	..	1149	..	1158	..	12 19	..	1228
Addiscombe C .... arr	....	1017	..	..	1035	..	..	..	..	11 1	....	..	..	1131	..	..	..	12 1	....	..	..	1231
Bingham Road	..	..	1021	..	..	..	..	1053	..	..	..	1121	..	..	..	1151	..	..	..	12 21	..	..
Coombe Road	....	..	1024	..	..	..	..	1056	..	..	....	1124	..	..	..	1154	..	..	....	12 24	..	..
Selsdon	..	..	1026	..	..	..	..	1058	..	..	..	1126	..	..	..	1157	..	..	..	12Z30	..	..
Sanderstead .. .. arr	....	..	1029	..	..	..	..	11 0	..	..	....	1129	..	..	..	..	..	..	....	12 33	..	..

BR Passenger Services Southern Region, May 23-September 25 1949

Below:
Work on the ac conversion of the lines from Balham to Coulsdon North and Selhurst to Sutton was in hand when World War 1 broke out in 1914. Afterwards the work continued on civil engineering and overhead line work, but little progress was made with rolling stock until the Southern Railway took over — ac electric services to Coulsdon North and Wallington finally commenced on 1 April 1925. For these were used five-car formations with two driving trailers and two trailers, with a motor luggage van as third vehicle in each 'unit'. There were 60 driving trailers (20 composite, 40 third) and 20 trailer composites, mostly built at Lancing; the remainder came from Eastleigh or contractors.

Twenty-one motor luggage vans were constructed by the Metropolitan Carriage Wagon & Finance Co in 1923-4. Here is No 10114, built in January 1924, seen in Coulsdon sidings. After its ac life was over, it was rebuilt in March 1934 as bogie goods brake No 56267, retaining much of the original side panelling. Some of these survived until the 1970s, the last few in Engineer's trains. *Ian Allan Library*

Below:
Coulsdon and Wallington stock in Coulsdon North sidings, on 27 May 1927. The 'CW' stock had a little more than two years to run before the ac system was switched off and dismantled, replaced by the dc third rail system which the Southern had decided to standardise on. The last ac trains ran on 22 September 1929. The carriages, however, survived, converted to dc operation and playing a major part in the Southern's suburban work until the end of the 1950s.
*Ian Allan Library/
Madgwick Collection*

Electric Stock in Use Between 1909 and 1962

These notes are a summary of the electric multiple-unit stock used on the Southern lines between 1909 and 1962. They are not exhaustive, giving only the numbers of units and of the coaches used in them; for reasons of space the coach numbers are not given in full allocated order, which was often quite complex and subject to changes.

The LB&SCR built, converted, or bought from contractors, 40 coaches for the South London Line electrification (of which eight were transferred to steam work and later returned to electric use by the SR) and 100 for the Crystal Palace routes. It also built or ordered a number of coaches for the Coulsdon/Wallington scheme, but some of those were never used on electric services. Its electric coaches (including those intended for electric work but used on steam services) were allocated Nos 3201-304 and 4001-138. The Southern Railway numbered the ac stock in the series 8567-616, 9169-88, 9655-74 and 9811-914; the motor vans built for the Coulsdon-Wallington electrification were SR Nos 10101-21; the LB&SC seems not to have decided how to number them.

The LB&SCR coded its electric stock according to the route(s) it was designed for; thus the South London stock became 'SL', Crystal Palace stock 'CP', and the Coulsdon/Wallington (ie Sutton) stock was to be 'CW'.

The L&SWR's stock comprised 84 three-car multiple-units, numbered E1-E84, converted from steam stock in 1914-17, and 24 two-car trailer sets, numbered T1-24, converted from steam stock in 1921-2. There was also the Waterloo & City line stock. No stock codes were used: an eight-car train was '8' in the stock working schedules, and remained '8' after the SR took over.

Eventually the Southern Railway devised its own coding system, but not until 1932, when '4LAV' became the first of many codes, mostly of one figure and three letters, describing electric and, later, diesel-electric multiple-units and trailer sets — but not the Waterloo & City stock.

The Southern Railway/Southern Region multiple-unit type codes indicate the general type and formation of the motor units for operating purposes and do not distinguish between sub-types. They are listed below, in unit number series order, with the building dates and periods in which most of them ran, and the car numbers originally built or converted for their type. The Southern used the word 'car' — eg, two-car unit — interchangeably with 'coach' for the electric vehicles, whilst using the word 'carriage' as a general description for anything that was not a loco, wagon or van; the unit codes could be printed with a hyphen, or without. All units were motored; by convention, an unmotored formation was a 'set'. For space reasons, the details set out here are a summary only. Coaches were not necessarily allocated in numerical order; war damage, accidents and augmentation to four-car form resulted in exchanges between units, especially the 1201-1800 series and the 4COR/RES/BUF stock.

The SR referred to its coaches as thirds, composites, firsts, third brakes, composite brakes, etc. Motor coaches were, for example, motor third brake; electric trailers were simply 'third', etc; driving trailers were (usually) 'driving trailer composite'; saloons had the word 'saloon' added before the description, which was painted in full on the solebar.

Stock Code

two-car trailer set, nine sub-types, series
989-1200; converted from L&SWR,
SE&CR or LB&SCR steam stock, and
LB&SCR ac electric stock in 1920-37,
withdrawn 1941-8. Car numbers 8901-
9300, 9825-30, 10401-18.

three-car suburban unit, various sub-
types, series 1201-801 (No 1801
renumbered 1600); converted or new
1914-37, augmented to 4SUB or
withdrawn 1942-9. Except for Nos 1285-
310 and 1496-524, all augmentations
were renumbered in random order. The
various batches of these units were:

Nos 1201-84, the LSWR units converted
from steam stock in 1914-17; cars MTB
Nos 8001-126, MCB Nos 8751-92, TC
Nos 9351-434. Most augmented to
Nos 4131-71/95-4234 in 1942-8.
Nos 1285-310, built new for the
Guildford/Dorking scheme in 1925;
cars MTB Nos 8127-78, TC Nos 9435-60.
Augmented to Nos 4300-25 in 1945-6.
Nos 1401-95/1525-34, converted from
SECR steam stock in 1925-6; cars MTB
Nos 8227-416, MTB Nos 9485-579.
Most augmented into 4431-594 series in
1946-9.
Nos 1496-524, built new for the Eastern
section in 1925; cars MTB Nos 8417-74,
TC Nos 9580-608. Augmented to
Nos 4326-54 in 1945-6.
Nos 1525-34, as No 1401 etc, additional
in 1926; cars MTB Nos 8475-94, TC
Nos 9609-18. Augmented to same series
as No 1401 etc.
Nos 1579-99, additional units converted
from LSWR steam stock in 1932-7; cars
MTB Nos 9789-800, 9831-60, TC
Nos 9609-18, 9671-4, 9759-75. Most
augmented into 4401-594 series.
Nos 1600 (ex-1801) and 1797-800,
converted from LB&SCR steam stock
in 1932; cars MTB Nos 8586-95, TC
Nos 9666-70; some augmented into
4580-614 series.
Nos 1601-30, converted from SE&CR
steam stock in 1927-28; cars MTB

Nos 8495-554, TC Nos 9619-48. Most
augmented into 4431-516 series.
Nos 1631-57, converted from LB&SCR
steam stock in 1928-9; cars MTB
Nos 8617-70, TC Nos 9675-701. Mostly
augmented into 4517-614 series.
Nos 1658-701, converted from L&SWR
steam stock in 1927-8; cars MTB 8179-
222, MCB Nos 8793-836, 9307-50. Most
augmented into 4172-94 and 4235-50
series.
Nos 1702-16 as No 1631 Lot, converted
in 1928; cars MTB Nos 8671-85, MCB
Nos 8837-51, TC Nos 9702-16. Most
augmented into 4517-614 series.
Nos 1717-72, converted from ac electric
stock 1929-30; cars MTB Nos 8686-749,
MCB Nos 8852-900, TC Nos 9461-83,
9717-49, MCB Nos 9801-07. Most
augmented into 4517-79 series.
Withdrawn 1955-60; underframes of
these units were unsuitable for further
use, being ex-AC-electric (ie, not SR
standard). (Note: Nos 1601-772 were all
for Central section)
Nos 1773-90 (in 1930-1) and 1791-96 (in
1932), additional units converted from
L&SWR steam stock; cars MTB
Nos 8223-6, 8555-95, TC Nos 9301-6,
9484, 9649-70, MCB Nos 9807-17/22-4.
Most augmented into 4517-614 series.

The carriage number series 8001-900, 9301-824,
9831-999 used by the SR for the above three-car
units and also for the 2SL, 2WIM and 2NOL
units, was divided as follows: Nos 8001-749
motor brake thirds; 8751-900 motor composite
brakes, 9301-749, 9759-75 and 9801-17 trailer
compos, 9751-8 and 9781-800 motor third
brakes, 9818-24 motor compo brakes, 9831-910
motor third brakes, 9912-99 driving trailer
compos (except 9951-4, driving trailer thirds).
All suburban composites became third class in
October 1941, and third class became second
class in June 1956.
   Nos 8750, 9750, 9776-80 and 9911 were left
vacant. Some numbers had been previously
used for ac electric stock in 1923-9 and others
were used again for rebuilt or new 4SUB
coaches in 1949-51. Note that the carriage
numbers of rebuilt SUB coaches had no

connection with the numbers of the coaches from which they were rebuilt.

2SL   two-car South London line units, Nos 1801-8 (numbered 1901-8 until 1934); built 1909 as ac, altered to dc 1929, ran until 1954. Cars: MTB Nos 8723-30, DTC Nos 9751-58.

2WIM two-car Wimbledon-West Croydon line units, Nos 1809-12 (numbered 1909-12 until 1934); built 1909 as ac, used as main line steam stock 1912-30, altered to dc 1930, ran until 1954. Cars: MCB Nos 9818-21, DTT Nos 9951-4.

2NOL two-car non-lavatory units, 1813-90 (converted from steam 1934-6, withdrawn 1957-9); batches: Nos 1813-62 (MTB Nos 9861-910, DTC Nos 9940-50/64/65/ 63/62/61); Nos 1863-82 (MTB Nos 8596-615, DTC Nos 9920-39) and 1883-90 (MTB Nos 9781-88, DTC Nos 9913-18/12/19).

2BIL two-car lavatory units, Nos 2001-152, lavatory in both coaches (1935/38-69/71); cars: MTB Nos 10567-718, DTC Nos 12034-185, 12854-6/7/8 (units Nos 2001-48 were numbered 1891-99, 1890, 1901-20/54-71 when new).

2HAL two-car lavatory units, Nos 2601-700, lavatory in one coach (most withdrawn 1969-71); cars: MTB Nos 10719-810, 12664, DTC Nos 12186-231, 12801-53/5.

4LAV four-car units with one lavatory coach, Nos 2921-55 — most withdrawn 1968; cars: MTB Nos 10497-566, TC 11501-35, side corridor lavatory TC Nos 11999-12033. (units Nos 2921-53 were numbered 1921-53 until early in 1937).

6PUL six-car unit with Pullman car, Nos 3001-20 (originally 2001 etc, coded 6COR); built 1932, ran 1933-66; gangwayed within unit; lavatories in trailers; cars: 40 saloon MTB of series 11001-46; TC Nos 11751-90; TT Nos 10001-20; 20 of the 23 Pullman trailer composites Nos 256-78.

6PAN six-car unit with pantry car, Nos 3021-37 (originally 2021-37); built 1935, ran until 1966; gangwayed within unit; lavatories in all trailers; cars: saloon MTB Nos 11047-80, (not in numerical order); TT Nos 10021-54, TF Nos 12260-76, pantry cars Nos 12501-17. War loss No 10039 was replaced (by new one, same number) in 1946.

6CIT six-coach unit with Pullman car, 3041-43 (originally 2041 etc, coded 6COR); built 1931-2, ran 1933-66; cars: saloon MTB Nos 11001-2, 11015-16, trailer Nos 11041-2; firsts 12251-9; three of the 23 Pullman trailer composites 256-78. Nos 12251-9 derated to thirds and compos *circa* 1941-5 and renumbered by 1946 to 10113-5, 11862-7 (not in order).

5BEL five-coach all-Pullman unit, Nos 3051-53 (originally 2051 etc, coded 5PUL); built 1932, ran 1933-73; cars: Pullman MTB Nos 88-93, Pullman trailer thirds 85-7, six Pullman trailer firsts.

4RES four-coach unit, gangwayed throughout, with restaurant facilities, Nos 3054-72; built 1937. Saloon MTB Nos 11139-76; diner firsts 12231-49; kitchen thirds ('restaurant') No 12601-19. The diner and kitchen cars were delivered late, needing more work done by the SR, and so were not allocated in numerical order. Equivalent of three units lost in World War 2. 4RES operation as such ceased January 1964 surviving units reformed as 4PUL and withdrawn in that form 1965-6. No 3072 altered to buffet in 1955.

4GRI 4RES type with kitchen car altered to griddle car circa 1961-2 (renumbered 3086-8 in 1964 and withdrawn 1971)

4BUF four-coach unit, gangwayed throughout, with buffet car, Nos 3073-85 (built 1938, ran until 1971); cars: saloon MTB Nos 11229-54; trailer compos 11846-57; buffet cars 12518-30.

4COR four-coach unit, corridor throughout, Nos 3101-58 (built 1937-8/45/46, ran until 1971). Cars: saloon MTB Nos 11081-138, 177-11228; trailer thirds Nos 10055-109, trailer compos Nos 11791-845.

25 COR, RES and BUF vehicles, including two diner firsts and three kitchen cars, lost by war damage and replaced by new vehicles in 1945-6/48: 11 motor third brakes, seven trailer thirds; five trailer compos, one buffet car, one diner first were built, all with the old numbers and identical with the originals. The postwar reforming added units Nos 3156-58 to the 4COR list. Spare coaches left after the RES and 4PUL formations were withdrawn were formed up as units Nos 3159-68.

4DD four-coach double-deck unit, Nos 4001-2 (later 4901-2); cars: MTB Nos 13001-4; trailers Nos 13501-4.

4SUB four-car suburban units, many variants, numbers in series 4101-754, built all-new, or new bodies on older underframes, or formed by augmentation of three-car units from 1941 to 1951; operated 1941-81. Some unit numbers used twice. Some trailers rewired and formed into 4EPB units between 1951 and 1957, with others into revised formations *circa* 1980-1. The main lots of 4SUB units were:

Nos 4101-10 all-new, completed 1941-5 (the 'Sheba' stock); cars: MTB Nos 10941-60, trailer thirds Nos 10419-28, trailer compos Nos 11471-80 (only No 11481 was ever fitted out as compo, remainder were always third/second).
Nos 4111-30 all-new, completed 1946; cars: MTB Nos 10961-1000, trailers 10429-48, 11481-500. Nos 10981-1000 and 10439-48 were 'small saloon' type.
Nos 4131-250 augmented mostly from 1201 and 1658 series units, using trailers from two-car trailer sets. Most withdrawn 1954-7.
Nos 4250-7 formed from cars spare after accidents and war damage; withdrawn mid-1950s.
Nos 4277-99 all-new, completed 1948-9;

cars: MTB Nos 10849-94, trailers Nos 10121-66.
Nos 4300-54 augmented from 1285-310 and 1496-524 using a new trailer in each unit; new cars: Nos 10346-400. Withdrawn 1959-62.
Nos 4355-77 completed 1947-8; cars: MTB Nos 10895-940, trailers in 102xx and 114xx series.
Nos 4378-87 completed 1948; cars: saloon MTB Nos 10829-48, trailers Nos 10472-81, saloon trailers Nos 12351-60.
Nos 4401-516 (1946-7), 4517-94 and some in series 4601-14 augmented 1946-9, from units in series 1401-800, using a new trailer in each unit; many car exchanges and reforms. New cars in series 10167-345, 10449-71 and 11448-70. Most withdrawn 1949-57.
Nos 4601-07 saloon MTB (Nos 12650-63) new in 1950 with trailers of 1946-8 builds. Nos 4617-20 formed 1972-6 using cars of 1946-50 builds.
Nos 4621-754 to traffic 1949-51; mostly new bodies on old frames, some cars all new, one trailer in each of Nos 4667-754 taken from augmented units. Cars — new bodies: saloon MTB Nos 8616-55 and 11301-92; trailers Nos 8901-46, saloon trailers 8947-9034 and 12361-406; ex-augmentation trailers from series 10167-400/449-71 and 11448-70.

4EPB four-car suburban units with electro-pneumatic brake and 'buckeye' couplings, numbers originally in series 5001-370 (1951-95). The sub-series of 4EPB units were as follows; trailer car numbers were allocated in batch blocks, not in the sequence summarised here; some were saloon, some compartment:

Nos 5001-53, SR rebuilds, completed 1951-4; saloon MTB 14001-106, trailers 15001-33 (ex-4SUB stock rewired and renumbered) and 15101-53/59-78;
Nos 5101-260, SR rebuilds, completed 1953-7; saloon MTB Nos 14201-520, trailers 15034-78 (ex-4SUB stock rewired and renumbered), Nos 15154-58/79-15448. Nos 5301-70, BR standard

(but trailers of 5301-2 were SR ex-4SUB). Saloon MTB Nos 61516-623/25/26, 61989-2016, trailers Nos 70375-482, 70667-94.

In later years major facelifting, or reforming of existing coaches to deal with accident losses or the phasing out of compartment stock, produced units Nos 5261-64, 5401-97, and in 55xx and 56xx series.

2EPB two-car suburban unit with electro-pneumatic brake and 'buckeye' couplings, numbers originally Nos 5651-84, 5701-95, 5800 (completed 1954-60, last withdrawals 1995). Nos 5651-84 were on SR under-frames, with saloon MTB, Nos 14557-90, saloon driving trailers Nos 16101-34. Nos 5701 etc were BR standard, with saloon MTB Nos 61624, 65300-92, 65435, driving trailers (part saloon) Nos 77100-14, 75636, 77500-578. No 5781-95 were initially allocated to Tyneside and came to the Southern Region in 1963.

2HAP two-car lavatory unit with electro-pneumatic brake and 'buckeye' couplings, numbers originally 5601-36 on SR underframes, Nos 6001-173 BR standard (completed 1957-63); last withdrawals 1992; some BR HAPs were downgraded to run as suburban units, numbered in 59xx; towards the end, some were were coupled to run as four-car suburban units in 32xx, 33xx, and ran thus until 1995.

Nos 5601-36 had saloon MBS Nos 14521-56 and side corridor driving trailer composites Nos 16001-36. Nos 6001 etc were BR standard, with saloon MBS Nos 61241-303, 61648-88, 61872, 61962-88, 65393-434, and driving trailer composites Nos 75361-423, 75700-40, 75995-6021, 77115-56.

4CEP four-car corridor unit, originally Nos 7101-211 (completed 1956-63)

4BEP four-car corridor unit with buffet car, originally Nos 7001-22 (completed 1956-61). BEP units have now all gone, but many CEP units, BR Class 411, rebuilt and renumbered, are still in traffic. Car numbers originally allocated were:

CEP: motor brakes Nos 61033-40, 61229-40, 61404-89, 61694-791, 61868-71, 61948-61; trailer compos Nos 70037-40/43/44, 70235-40, 70303-45, 70552-600, 70653-9; trailer seconds Nos 70033-36, 70229-34/41/42, 70260-302, 70503-51, 70660-6. BEP: motor brakes 61041-4, 61390-409, 61792-811; trailer compos Nos 70041-2, 70346-55, 70601-10; buffet cars Nos 69000-21

MLV one-car motor luggage van, car numbers 68001-10; no unit numbers; built 1959-61. Now withdrawn.

Left:
The 1909 South London units included a trailer first; when the units were reformed *c*1910-12, the firsts were not needed and were transferred to main line steam work. In 1930 all eight were converted to dc electric. As units No 1909-12 they were sent to the newly electrified Wimbledon-West Croydon line; in 1934 they were renumbered 1809-12, coded 2WIM, and ran on the line until 1954. This view shows No 1811 passing Waddon Marsh Halt, which will become part of the Croydon Tramlink system in 1999. The gasworks has gone completely, replaced by an industrial estate. *G. Waterer*

Below left:
Towards the end of their life, the 2WIM units were helped out by the South London 2SL units Nos 1801-08. Seen here is the 12.32 Wimbledon to West Croydon at Mitcham with unit No 1805 on 23 October 1954. Days later this unit was on its way to the breakers' yard.
Ian Allan Library/J. J. Smith

Below:
Standard 2EPB units replaced the South London and Wimbledon-West Croydon stock. Here is No 5712 at Mitcham, in almost the same position as No 1805. This station will become a Tramlink stop. *Ian Allan Library/R. C. Riley*

Right:
Electrification opened on the Hounslow loop on 12 March 1916. L&SWR unit No E2 departs from Hounslow for Waterloo via Richmond. *G. Waterer Collection*

Below right:
In 1913 the L&SWR announced its scheme to electrify the lines from Waterloo to Wimbledon via East Putney, the Hounslow and Kingston 'loops' and the branches to Hampton Court and Shepperton, using the 600V dc third rail system. The first section opened was Waterloo to Wimbledon via East Putney, on 25 October 1915, and despite wartime problems, all the planned routes were operating by 18 June 1916. This was to be the start of the largest third rail dc system anywhere in the world.

L&SWR unit No E40 passes Cromer Road box between East Putney and Southfields on a down train from Waterloo to Wimbledon. *G. Waterer Collection*

Below:

The L&SWR electric rolling stock was converted from steam stock at Eastleigh carriage works, and totalled 84 three-car units, each with two driving motor brakes and an intermediate trailer. The L&SWR numbered them E1-E84; the Southern numbers were 1201-84. This formation, with minor variations in first and third class provision, was adopted as standard by the Southern Railway until 1939, by which time there were 466 three-car units in the suburban area. Of those three-car units, 55, numbered 1285-310 and 1496-524, were built new in 1925; all the remainder, given numbers 1401-95, 1525-34, 1579-801, were based on converted steam stock of L&SWR, LB&SCR or SE&CR origin, or on ac electric stock. The trailer sets, numbered 989-1200, were also all of 'steam' or ac origin.

This massive fleet covered the electrification of Western section routes to Guildford (via Cobham) and Dorking in 1925, Eastern section lines from Victoria and Holborn Viaduct to Crystal Palace (High Level) and Orpington, also in 1925, and in 1926 the Charing Cross/Cannon Street services to Addiscombe, Hayes, Bromley North and routes to Dartford. 1928 saw Central section electric services to Caterham and Tattenham Corner, and from London Bridge to Crystal Palace via Sydenham. 1929 dc electrification covered the rest of the Central section and saw out the last ac trains. In 1930 the suburban area was virtually completed with electric services to Windsor, Gravesend Central, and between Wimbledon and West Croydon. The remainder of the 466 three-car units, and the two-car trailer sets which were worked with them, were for extra services, and minor additions such as Woodside-Sanderstead in 1935.

Also part of the suburban fleet were some two-car units, classified 2NOL, of motor third brake plus driving trailer composite. These were given numbers 1813-90. About 40 of them were used on main line or other non-London services, but Nos 1851-90 spent most of their life in the suburbs.

The L&SWR units, themselves rebuilt from steam stock, were rebuilt by the Southern between 1934 and 1940. Here unrebuilt three-car unit No 1201 is at Clapham Junction (Platform 10) bound for Waterloo. *G. Waterer Collection*

Left:
Also at Clapham Junction (Platform 9); this is a rebuilt unit, originally No E25, then No 1225, but by this time augmented to four cars as 4SUB No 4208, on a down race special sometime in the 1950s, probably to Esher (for Sandown Park). *G. Waterer*

Top:
In 1939 the Southern Railway decided that the practice, begun by the L&SWR in 1922, of making up eight-car suburban trains from two three-car units flanking a two-car trailer set was unsatisfactory. The three-car units were to be made up to four cars using suitable trailers from two-car trailer sets, or by building new coaches. Some three-car units and many coaches from trailer sets would be withdrawn, replaced by new four-car units or by stock with new bodywork on existing underframes. The war delayed the programme, but by 1947 it was in full swing and for the next dozen years the Southern suburban scene was enlivened by a variety of mixed formations including new steel-bodied coaches in old units, sometimes themselves including bodywork of more than one pre-Grouping company. Photographs of some of these units are rare.

All the four-car suburban units, regardless of whether they were new, rebuilt, old or mixed, were designated 4SUB. The augmented units were numbered 4131-257, 4300-54, 4401-594, 4601-08/10/13/14. Some did not last long before they were withdrawn. Some numbers were used twice. Another ex-L&SWR unit, 4SUB No 4207, passes the former Midland Railway and London & North Western Railway depot at Peckham Rye, bound for London Bridge.
Ian Allan Library/R. C. Riley

Above:
Rebuilt L&SWR unit, No S4151 with post-nationalisation 'S' prefix and large figures, at Clapham Junction (Platform 15) leaving for West Croydon *c*1948-9. The side of the motor coach also bore the legend 'British Railways'.
G. Waterer Collection

Right:
4SUB unit No 4246, with one original L&SWR motor coach and the other three coaches converted from steam stock in the late 1920s, leaves Waterloo for Shepperton from Platform 16 sometime in 1954. This platform was on the site of 'Eurostar' Platform 20. *L. A. Mack*

Below right:
Three-coach suburban unit No 1679, newly converted by the SR from L&SWR steam stock, at Selhurst depot in 1928.
Ian Allan Library

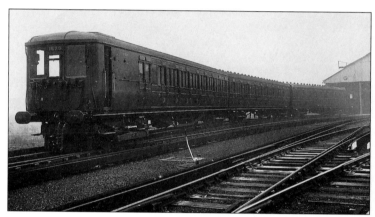

Below:
At Hampton Court in May 1949 is 4SUB unit No 4161. Note the labels on the compartment windows; the one next to the guard's van reads 'Ladies Only'; the other is 'No Smoking' and was the exception, not the rule; how times have changed!
G. Waterer Collection

Left:
At London Bridge, Platform 4, showing the old middle line, known as 'No 5 line', still in position, with Platforms 6 and 7 adjacent. 4SUB unit No 4412, augmented from a three-car L&SWR-based unit with a late 1940s steelbodied trailer, is about to depart to Dartford via Sidcup. *G. Waterer Collection*

Below left:
The last three-car suburban units converted from L&SWR steam stock by the SR were Nos 1579-84, in 1937. In 4SUB form they were Nos 4424-29; here, coach No 9798 of unit No 4428 (ex-1583) is at Forest Hill on 6 August 1950. *G. Waterer*

Below:
Among the oddities turned out by the SR was this motor brake, No 9815; it had a lengthened L&SWR steam body on an ex-Brighton ac electric type underframe (which never actually saw ac service); it was in three-car unit No 1780, augmented to 4SUB No 4573, and ended its days in 1959 as No 4501 (the second one with that number). Here it is at Hampton Court. *G. Waterer*

Above:
A pre-1939 photo taken between Bromley South and Bickley of an Orpington-bound 6BIL-plus-2NOL. This stock was allocated to the Eastern Section for a peak hour Sevenoaks to Cannon Street and return train, the 'Waldron Smithers train', named (unofficially) after the MP for Orpington. The motor third is No 9897, in unit No 1849, and the side route board reads 'Penge Beckenham Bromley South Orpington'. These boards were general until 1939, and reappeared briefly on some lines in 1946. Some were eventually used by Lancing for carriage body repairs.
Ian Allan Library

Above right:
One of the regular services for the coastal NOLs Nos 1813-50 was Brighton-West Worthing. Here No 1829 is at Hove on 31 August 1955. *L. A. Mack*

Right:
Another coastal NOL duty was Brighton-Horsted Keynes. Here No 1821 departs from Brighton on the 5.12pm to Horsted Keynes, also in 1955. *G. Waterer*

Above:
Still in coastal NOL territory, at Hastings, a Brighton-bound via Eastbourne train with No 1822 leading. Note the position of the ground signals. *G. Waterer*

Left:
For their whole working life, the Waterloo-Alton/Portsmouth & Southsea stopping service was the preserve of the 2BIL units, but NOL units frequently deputised. Here, NOL No 1833 is on a down train, passing Clapham Junction on 26 June 1955. Where are those two 12-year-old spotters now? *L. A. Mack*

Left:
At Wandsworth Road on the South London line in 1954, bound for Victoria, 2NOL No 1870, which spent almost the whole of its life in the London area; the headcode is still in position on the rear. *G. Waterer*

Right:
2NOL No 1867 leads an empty stock train about to depart Waterloo for Farnham depot via Brentford and Ascot on a Saturday morning in July 1954. This stock returned to Waterloo after cleaning, calling at Aldershot and Woking, only for conveyance of army personnel, arriving at Waterloo just in time for the mid-day peak which was then still a feature of Saturday life. *L. A. Mack*

Below right:
A pair of NOL units at Beckenham Junction with No 1852 leading, about to depart to Victoria via Crystal Palace in 1954. The sidings were removed some years later; their site will be used for the Croydon Tramlink terminus. *G. Waterer*

Below:
An unidentified South Eastern unit passes Honor Oak Park on a Charing Cross to Tattenham Corner service.
G. Waterer Collection

Left:
Three-car unit No 1601 is about to depart from London Bridge (Low Level) for Tattenham Corner. *G. Waterer Collection*

Below left:
Most of the 1401, 1525 and 1601 series units were augmented to 4SUB, using new steel-bodied trailers, in 1946-7 and 1949. Augmented South Eastern unit No 4465 (ex-three-car No 1447) is at Hampton Court in May 1949. *G. Waterer Collection*

Below:
Approaching East Croydon from the south on 30 April 1950, South Eastern unit No 4492, with its steel-bodied trailer recently replaced by a wooden-bodied coach from No 4448.
G. Waterer Collection

Right:
South Eastern unit No 4493 leaves Cannon Street for Dartford via Bexleyheath.
G. Waterer Collection

Below right:
South Eastern 4SUB unit No 4517 is seen here in Platform 9 at London Bridge Low Level. This platform was removed when London Bridge station was rebuilt in the 1970s, but until then could be used for South Eastern section trains. The headcode P, with a bar over it, indicated that the train was bound for Gravesend or Gillinghham via Blackheath and Woolwich.
G. Waterer Collection

Below:
At Charing Cross on 6 October 1951, South Eastern 4SUB unit No 4580 is ready to leave for Hayes via Lewisham, while 'LBSC' 4SUB No 4561 carries the headcode for Sevenoaks.
G. Waterer Collection

Left:
At Strawberry Hill on 3 October 1953 is 'Brighton' 4SUB No 4251, newly ex-Selhurst shops where it has had its biennial coat of varnish. It was augmented with an LBSC-type trailer in the war years before construction of steel-bodied trailers had begun. *L. A. Mack*

Below left:
On the South Eastern side of Peckham Rye station is 'Brighton' unit No 4539, on a Holborn Viaduct-Dartford service. *G. Waterer Collection*

Below:
At Clapham Junction on 8 November 1949, augmented 'Brighton' unit No 4564 heads a Chessington South train, while an up train of SR 1925 stock leaves for Waterloo and a 2NOL unit is visible on the Windsor side. The motor brakes of No 4564 were later to become a towing unit, taking withdrawn units from Durnsford Road depot to Strawberry Hill depot for stripping and despatch to the breakers' yard. *Ian Allan Library/C. B. Herbert*

Right:
At New Cross Gate, No 4512 (the second one of that number, it was a reform of surviving 'Brighton' coaches after the steel-bodied trailers had been taken for EPB use) is bound for Epsom Downs sometime in 1958. A 4COR unit can be seen in the south sidings, which are now all removed.
L. A. Mack

Right:
At Wimbledon, another 'Brighton' re-form, No 4506, is bound for Chessington South.
Ian Allan Library/ J. C. Beckett

Below:
At Hampton Court station, another reform from the last days of the 'Brighton' stock, 4SUB No 4513.
Ian Allan Library/ B. A. Haresnape

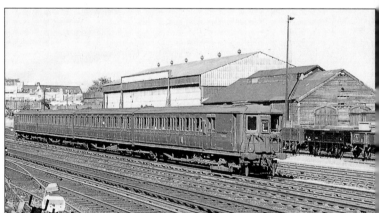

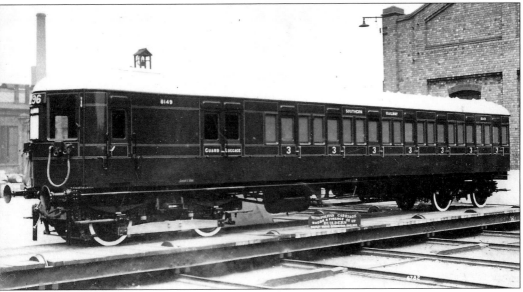

Top:
Old and — in the early 1950s when this shot was taken — at Waterloo in the early 1950s — 4SUB units Nos 4254 and 4127. No 4254 was another Southern oddity with a 'Brighton' motor and trailer, a 'South Eastern' trailer, and a 'South Western' motor, No 9876, which when first converted had been part of a 2NOL unit. *L. A. Mack*

Above:
Southern Railway 'Guildford/Dorking' motor third brake No 8149, of unit No 1296 (later 4311), is seen here at its 'photo opportunity' at Met Carriage Wagon & Finance Co. when new in 1925.
G. Waterer Collection

Top:
From the late 1930s onwards, the Guildford/Dorking units could be found anywhere on the suburban network. Here is 4SUB No 4320, which by this time had acquired a trailer from the Eastern Section's Orpington line units of 1925, as the rear unit of the 6.49pm (SX) Charing Cross to Gillingham, pulling away from Waterloo on 1 June 1959.
Ian Allan Library/C. Haydon

Above:
'SUB' units could often be found outside the suburban area in the 1950s. Here is No 4309 at Woking on an up service to Waterloo — the reporting label on the cab window means it is probably a Farnborough airshow extra from Aldershot. *G. Waterer*

Above:
4SUB No 4306 leads a down Alton through Clapham Junction. *G. Waterer*

Below:
No 4309 again, this time departing from Victoria Central section side for Beckenham Junction. Note the siding between Platforms 9 (Central) and 8 (South Eastern). No 4309 became a popular target for photographers in 1958, when it somehow acquired a second steel-bodied trailer. *Ian Allan Library*

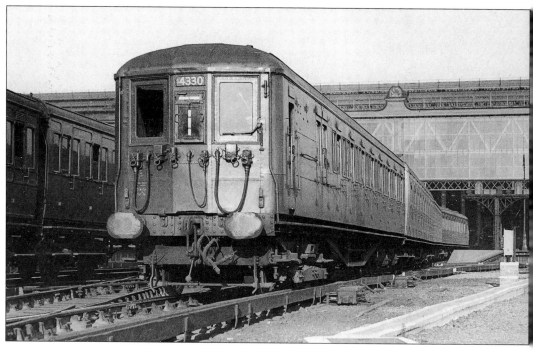

Top:
No 4330 of the 1925 Eastern section batch leaves Waterloo for Effingham Junction on 14 November 1949. At this time it still has its original small suburban buffers; in 1952/3 the series was fitted with the heavier 'Pullman' type.
Ian Allan Library/C. C. B. Herbert

Above:
Easter Monday races at Kempton Park meant single line working on the Shepperton branch; No 4332 collects the single line token at Sunbury on 19 April 1954. *Ian Allan Library/J. N. Faulkner*

Above:
An ordinary day's working: 4SUB No 4338 leads a London Bridge-Coulsdon North train at South Croydon. *Ian Allan Library*

Below:
4SUB No 4342 on a Holborn Viaduct to West Croydon train passing Camberwell box. In the 1950s, stock workings into and out of Holborn Viaduct often involved swaps between the Eastern and Central sections; the same could happen at Dorking and it was not unknown for a 4SUB to work out of the Windsor side of Waterloo in the morning and finish the day at Slade Green depot.
Ian Allan Library/R. C. Riley

Top:
4SUB No 4347 on a Dartford-Holborn Viaduct train at Lewisham. *L. A. Mack*

Above:
Two 1925-type 4SUBs ready to leave London Bridge in the evening rush hour, one for Dartford, one for Addiscombe. Until the 1970s, all Eastern section down trains at London Bridge departed from Platforms 1, 2 and 3, and the route could be served from any of the three platfoms. *L. A. Mack*

Below:
Also on the Crystal Palace (HL) branch, on 27 August 1954, a few weeks before closure, is all-steel 4SUB No 4365 in the down platform at Honor Oak, leaving for Crystal Palace. The station site is now a housing estate. *G. Waterer Collection*

Bottom:
At Upper Sydenham on the same day (27 August 1954) is 4SUB No 4671 in the down platform. The tunnel is still there, now boarded up; the station master's house behind the trees still remains. *G. Waterer Collection*

Right:
With the virtual completion of the suburban network, the Southern Railway turned to main line conversion, starting with the Brighton line. On 23 January 1930, Sir Herbert Walker, General Manager of the Southern Railway, obtained the Board's approval for electrification from London to Brighton and West Worthing, and Redhill to Reigate, 52 route miles, with colour light signalling being installed over the 36 miles from Coulsdon North to Brighton — a record at that time.

The first stock into service was ready for service as far as Three Bridges, which started in July 1932. It was the 4LAV, which was really a high quality suburban unit. It had two motor third compartment brakes, a compartment trailer composite, and a side-corridor trailer composite with lavatory each end.

The Brighton-West Worthing locals were worked with three-car suburban units transferred from the London area until 1935, when they were replaced by 2NOL units which came with the rolling stock order for the Eastbourne scheme.The 4LAV units, Nos 2921-53, were the mainstay of the London to Brighton and Reigate semi-fast and slow services from 1933 until withdrawn in 1967-8. They had three compartment coaches and one side corridor composite. This view shows a compartment interior of a motor third brake in unit No 2921.
Ian Allan Library

Right:
A Victoria to Brighton slow, unit No 2947 leading, passes the old Gatwick Airport station, now completely gone.
Ian Allan Library/R. C. Riley

Top:
The London Bridge-Brighton slows alternated with the Victorias to give a half-hourly service south of Croydon. This is unit No 2923 at Three Bridges. Note the double colour lights instead of today's route indicators. *Ian Allan Library*

Above:
There were few 4LAV workings away from the London-Brighton main line. Ex-works 4LAV No 2951 is at Clapham Junction on the regular working of the 6.33am Ore to Victoria which commenced in July 1935 and ran until the early 1960s. *Ian Allan Library/P. J. Sharpe*

Right:
On 24 October 1947, the 7.33am Haywards Heath to London Bridge, with unit No 2926 in the rear, was run into by the 8.04am from Tattenham Corner. No 10511 of 2926, the motor brake, was written off. Here No 2926 is seen working a Victoria-Brighton service in the late 1950s. *Ian Allan Library*

Below right:
The replacement for No 10511 in 2926 was No 10764, taken from Medway 2HAL unit No 2646; here it is seen at the front of the 2.47pm Victoria to Brighton on 21 August 1960. *Ian Allan Library*

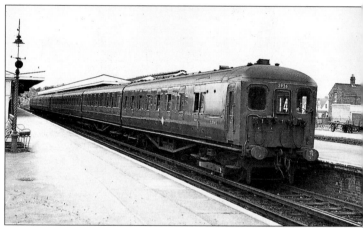

Below:
In 1939 the Southern decided that it need two more 4LAV units; Nos 2953/54 appeared after World War 2 started, in 1940. One of them pays a rare visit to Horsham on 10 October 1965. The 'mini yellow end' warning panel was introduced in 1963. *Ian Allan Library/J. Scrace*

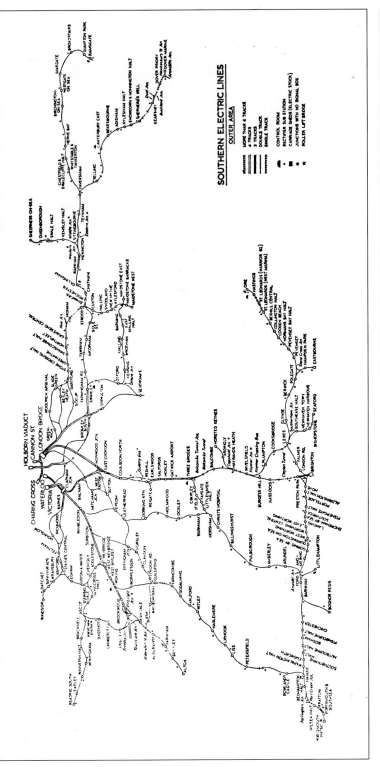

Southern Electric
outer area lines, summer
1959.

Route Indicators
for Electric Trains

Route indicators, in the form of letters on suburban stock, and numbers on main line stock, were adopted by the Southern Railway, based on L&SWR and LB&SCR practice. The 'Southern' headcodes listed here were those in use between July 1939 and the mid-1960s. Some have since changed or become obsolete; others were added when additional routes were electrified. Diesel electric units were brought into the system in 1957. Electric and diesel locos were also included for some years, but reverted to disc route codes.

ac Overhead System Headcodes, circa 1911 to 1929

1   Victoria and Crystal Palace via Streatham Hill

2   Victoria and Streatham Hill

2   Crystal Palace and Streatham Hill

3   Victoria and Norwood Junction via Streatham Hill & Crystal Palace

3   Empties Norwood Junction and Crystal Palace to work passr to Victoria

4   London Bridge and Crystal Palace via Tulse Hill

5   London Bridge and Victoria via Tulse Hill & Streatham Hill

6   London Bridge and Norwood Junction via Tulse Hill & Crystal Palace

6   Empties Norwood Junction and Crystal Palace before or after working London Bridge & Crystal Palace passenger

7   Victoria and Selhurst via Streatham Common

8   Victoria and West Croydon via Crystal Palace

9   Victoria and Sutton via Streatham Common

10   Victoria and East Croydon via Crystal Palace

11   Victoria and Coulsdon North via Streatham Common

12   Victoria and Coulsdon North via Crystal Palace

14   publicity photograph only

SL   Victoria and London Bridge via South London line (from 1925; previously, no code carried)

Headcodes Outside the General Arrangements

2   London Bridge and Victoria via South London Line

2   Wimbledon and West Croydon via Mitcham Junction

(Note: the number 2 as used for the foregoing two routes until the SL and WIM stock was withdrawn was a single character on a letter-style stencil and was regarded as a letter headcode.)

Letter Headcodes Listed in 'Southern' Instructions c1947-60

Empty trains of suburban stock to Durnsford Rd depot via Wimbledon 'C' Box or Ewell West from Waterloo, Chessington South, Dorking North, Effingham Junction, Hampton Court, Shepperton and Strawberry Hill, were to show a white blank with no bar or dot(s) above, viz: □. White blank □ was also to be shown for Waterloo to Wimbledon Park via East Putney. Some letter codes, mainly Eastern section, were one-way, hence the distinction between 'and' and 'to'.

H unmodified, ie, no bar or dots above letter

Cannon Street and Hayes via Lewisham	25
Charing Cross to Hayes via Lewisham	24
Holborn Viaduct and Herne Hill	75
London Bridge to Victoria via Tulse Hill and Streatham Hill	01
Orpington to Holborn Viaduct via Petts Wood and Herne Hill	71
Sevenoaks to Holborn c1938, altered later to code L	73
Staines and Windsor (attd or detd Waterloo-Weybridge via Brentford)	17
Tooting-Wimbledon-Mitcham-Bognor direct excursion	49
Victoria to Herne Hill	74
Waterloo and Hampton Court	30
Waterloo and Weybridge or Chertsey via Brentford	17
West Croydon and Dorking North	30

H with bar above letter H̄

Bickley to Holborn or Blackfriars via Catford	27
Cannon Street or Charing Cross to Hayes via Ladywell loop	34, 35
Hayes to Charing Cross via Lewisham	24
Sevenoaks to Holborn via Petts Wood and Nunhead	73
Staines and Windsor (attd or detd Waterloo-Weybridge via Richmond)	18
Tooting-Wimbledon-Mitcham-Littlehampton excursion	38
Victoria & Crystal Palace via Streatham Common, Selhurst and Norwood Junc	82
Virginia Water to Chertsey or Weybridge	18
Waterloo and Chertsey or Weybridge via Richmond	18
Waterloo and Effingham or Guildford via Cobham	43, 42

H with dot above letter Ḣ

Hayes to Cannon Street via Ladywell loop	35
Selhurst and West Croydon direct empties	03 bar
Selhurst depot and West Croydon via Selhurst empties	30 bar

Victoria & Wallington empties (coded J until about 1950)	30 bar
Victoria to London Bridge via Streatham Hill and Tulse Hill (also recorded as H unmod)	01
Waterloo to Weybridge via Brentford empties (from Nov 1954)	17 bar

H with two dots above letter Ḧ

Chertsey and stations on Hounslow Loop empties	17 bar
Crystal Palace High Level to Holborn	87
Durnsford Road depot to Hampton Court empties	30 bar
Effingham Junction and Guildford empties	42 bar
Hayes to Charing Cross via Ladywell Loop	34
London Bridge to Caterham via Forest Hill	81
Twickenham and Feltham empties	18 bar
Victoria and Streatham Hill empties	01 bar
Victoria to London Bridge via Streatham Hill and Tulse Hill	01
Waterloo to Weybridge via Brentford empties	18 bar (NOT 17 bar)
Waterloo and Windsor empties	58 bar
Waterloo to Hampton Court empties	30 bar or 31 bar

I unmodified, ie no bar or dots above letter

Cannon St and Beckenham Junction (later New Beckenham) via Lewisham	20, 21
Grove Park and Bromley North	1
Sanderstead or Selsdon to Cannon Street via Lewisham	29
Strood and Maidstone West	1
Victoria and Coulsdon North via Streatham Common	94
Waterloo and Horsham via Earlsfield and Epsom	17
Waterloo and Woking via Brentford and Ascot	25

I with bar above letter Ī

Beckenham Junction (later New Beckenham) to Charing Cross via Lewisham	20
Charing Cross or Cannon St to Beckenham Junction (later New Beckenham) via Ladywell Loop	30 & 31
Sanderstead or Selsdon to Charing Cross via Lewisham	28
Tattenham Corner and Selhurst depot empties	28 bar
Victoria and East Croydon via Selhurst	08
Victoria and Tattenham Corner via Selhurst	38
Waterloo and Effingham Junction via Earlsfield and Epsom	15 (not after June 1954)
Waterloo and Woking via Richmond and Ascot	26
Waterloo and Guildford via Earlsfield and Epsom	16

I with dot above letter İ

Beckenham Jc (later New Beckenham) to Cannon St via Ladywell Loop	31
Charing Cross or Cannon St to Sanderstead or Selsdon via Lewisham	28, 29
London Bridge and Coulsdon North via Forest Hill	05
Sanderstead or Selsdon to Cannon St via Ladywell Loop	39

I with double dot above letter Ï

Ascot and Farnham empties (1955-7)	92 bar
Beckenham Junction (later New Beckenham) to Charing Cross via Ladywell Loop	30
Charing Cross or Cannon St and Sanderstd or Selsdon via Ladywell Loop	38, 39
Chertsey to Waterloo via Weybridge and Wimbledon empties to work back passr	17bar
Durnsford Rd depot to Effingham Junction via Epsom empties (from 1954)	15 bar

London Bridge and Coulsdon North via Peckham Rye and Crystal Palace	not known
Victoria and Coulsdon North via Norbury empties	94 bar
Waterloo to Durnsford Rd depot via Wimbledon C box (from 1955)	01 bar
Waterloo to Worcester Park empties (from 1955)	01 bar

J unmodified, ie no bar or dots above letter

Gravesend or Dartford to Holborn Viaduct via Bexleyheath and Nunhead	79
Portsmouth and Gillingham via Epsom (special)	35
Specials between Central and Western sections	
Specials on Central section (inc suburban stock to main line destinations)	
Special workings on Western section (passenger or empty)	
Streatham or Tulse Hill and Brighton (Bank Holidays)	56
Waterloo and Ascot via Earlsfield, Weybridge and Sunningdale (special)	09

J with bar above letter J̄

Blackfriars or Holborn Viaduct to Gravesend via London Bridge and Bexleyheath (no equivalent 'up' letter code known)	79
Special workings on Central section (passenger or empty)	
Special workings on Western section (passenger or empty)	

J with dot above letter J̇

Blackfriars or Holborn Viaduct to Dartford via London Bridge and Bexleyheath	79
Gravesend or Dartford to Blackfriars via Bexleyheath and Nunhead	78
Orpington to Holborn Viaduct via London Bridge (no equivalent 'down' code known)	45
South Bermondsey and Brighton (Bank Holidays)	56

with two dots above letter J̈

Blackfriars or Holborn Viaduct to Gravesend via Nunhead and Bexleyheath   78

Special workings on Central section (passenger or empty)

Victoria and Brighton via Quarry, stopping or semifast   6

Western section empties to afterwork as J or J-with-bar (specials)

L unmodified, ie no bar or dots above letter

Ascot and Aldershot (attd or det Waterloo train via Brentford)   27

Ascot and Reading (special)   18

Cannon St and Dartford via Sidcup (not via Lewisham)   41

Charing Cross to Dartford via Sidcup (not via Lewisham)   40

Gravesend to Cannon Street via Sidcup   47

Gillingham to Cannon St via Dartford and Sidcup (not via Lewisham)   43

Holborn Viaduct and Bickley via Herne Hill   23

Special workings on Central section (passenger or empty)   various

Victoria or Blackfriars to Bickley via Herne Hill   24

Waterloo and Motspur Park or Chessington South   18

L with bar above letter L̄

Ascot and Aldershot attd or det train Waterloo via Richmond   28

Blackfriars to Bickley via Catford   29

Cannon St to Gillingham via Sidcup (not Lewisham)   43

Cannon St to Gravesend via Sidcup (not Lewisham)   47

Caterham and Purley empties   80 bar

Charing Cross and Gillingham via Sidcup (not Lewisham)   42

Charing Cross and Gravesend via Sidcup (not Lewisham)   46

Dartford to Charing Cross via Sidcup (not Lewisham)   40

Holborn Viaduct to Bickley via Catford   27

Sevenoaks to Blackfriars via Petts Wood and Herne Hill   61

Victoria and Caterham via Streatham Com and Purley   80

Victoria to Bickley via Catford   26

Waterloo and Epsom or Leatherhead   19

Waterloo and Reading via Richmond   28

Waterloo and Worcester Park   19

Waterloo to Effingham Junction via Epsom empties   15 bar

L with dot above letter L̇

Gravesend to Maidstone West det from Charing Cross via Sidcup train   46, 56

Blackfriars or Holborn Viaduct to Dartford via London Bridge and Sidcup   59

Cannon St and Dartford via Lewisham and Sidcup   51

Charing Cross to Dartford via Lewisham and Sidcup   50

Gillingham to Cannon St via Sidcup and Lewisham   53

London Bridge and Billingshurst via Mitcham Junction and Horsham spl   89

London Bridge and Horsham via Mitcham Junction and Dorking   89

Maidstone West to Cannon St via Sidcup & Lewisham   57

L with two dots above letter L̈

Ascot and Reading empties   18 bar

Blackfriars to Gravesend via London Bridge, Lewisham and Sidcup   59

Cannon St to Gillingham via Lewisham and Sidcup   53

Cannon St to Maidstone West trains between C/St and Gravesend   57

Charing Cross and Gillingham via Lewisham and Sidcup   52

Charing Cross and Maidstone West trains between Charing Cross and Gravesend   56

Dartford to Charing Cross via Sidcup and Lewisham	50
Durnsford Road depot and Chessington South empties	18 bar
London Bridge and Guildford via Mitcham Jc and Epsom	03

N unmodified, ie no bar or dots above letter

Blackfriars or Holborn Viaduct and Dartford via Nunhead & Blackheath	68
Crystal Palace and East Croydon special empties	3 bar
East Croydon to London Bridge via Sydenham	21
Gravesend to Blackfriars or Holborn Viaduct via Charlton Blackheath and Nunhead	68
Epsom Downs to Streatham Hill via Sutton, West Croydon and West Norwood (empties ex-race specials)	27 bar
Holborn Viaduct to West Croydon via Streatham, Streatham Common, Selhurst empties	79 bar
London Bridge-Wimbledon via Peckham Rye & Streatham empties	21 bar
Streatham Hill-Brighton via Quarry line	41
Waterloo-Aldershot or Farnham via Earlsfield	52
Waterloo-Ascot via Richmond race specials	51
Western section special workings	96

N with bar above letter N̄

Beckenham Junction to London Bridge via Crystal Palace and Tulse Hill — special empties	79 bar
Blackfriars or Holborn Viaduct to Gravesend via London Bridge and Blackheath/Charlton	69
Brighton to Eastbourne special empties	26 bar
Epsom-Fratton via Horsham special empties	53 bar
Gillingham to Waterloo E via Noth Kent line special	90
Hove and Portsmouth special passenger	60
London Bridge and Coulsdon North empties	20 bar

London Bridge and Wimbledon empties	81 bar
Selhurst and Epsom Downs via Sutton special empties	84 bar
Waterloo and Aldershot or Farnham via East Putney	53

N with dot above letter Ṅ

Blackfriars or Holborn Viaduct to Dartford via London Bridge, Blackheath and Charlton	69
Sanderstead or Hayes to Waterloo via Lewisham special	94
Waterloo and Alton via Earlsfield	32

N with two dots above letter N̈

Ascot race specials (empties)	51 bar
Blackfriars or Holborn Viaduct to Gravesend via Nunhead and Blackheath	68
London Bridge, Streatham Hill or Crystal Palace and Brighton via Quarry (Bank Holidays)	41
Waterloo and Alton via East Putney	02
Western section special workings (empties)	96, 98
Gravesend or Blackfriars or Holborn via Blackheath and London Bridge	69

O unmodified, ie no bar or dots above letter

Alton and Chertsey (passr to Woking, then empty)	none
Charing Cross or Cannon St to Orpington via Chislehurst (not via Lewisham)	12, 13
Elmers End and Hayes (in later years number was 04)	0
London Bridge and Ore via Eastbourne	61, 63
Orpington to Cannon St via Chislehurst (not Lewisham)	13
Strood and Gillingham	0
Victoria and Epsom Downs via Mitcham Junc	0
Waterloo and Alton via Earlsfield (Portsmth portion in rear)	12
Waterloo to Bognor Regis via Wimbledon and Horsham	67

Waterloo to Hounslow via Brentford empties	89 bar
Waterloo to Waterloo via Hounslow and Richmond	89
Woking to Alton (ex Waterloo-Portsmouth train)	12

O with bar above letter Ō

Blackfriars to Sevenoaks via Nunhead and Orpington	72
Chertsey and Farnham empties	15 bar
Epsom Downs to Victoria via Mitcham Jc empties	0 bar
Holborn Viaduct to Sevenoaks via Nunhead and Orpington	73
London Bridge and Ore direct	29
London Bridge and Epsom Downs via Streatham Mitcham Jc and Sutton — empties	53 bar
Orpington to Charing Cross via Chislehurst (not Lewisham)	12
Waterloo to Littlehampton via Wimbledon and Horsham	65
Waterloo to Waterloo via Richmond and Hounslow	87

O with dot above letter Ȯ

Orpington to Cannon St via Chislehurst and Lewisham	15
London Bridge to Epsom Dns via Norwd Jc and West Croydon	39
Victoria to Sevenoaks via Herne Hill and Orpington	70

O with two dots above letter Ö

Blackfriars to Sevenoaks via Herne Hill and Orpington	65
Cannon St to Orpington via Lewisham	15
Charing Cross and Orpington via Lewisham	14
Holborn Viaduct to Sevenoaks via Herne Hill and Orpington	71
Virginia Water or Chertsey and Woking empties	13 bar
Waterloo to Hounslow via Brentford empties	none
Waterloo and Bognor via Wimbledon, Horsham and Littlehampton	69

P unmodified, ie no bar or dots above letter

Blackfriars to Crystal Palace High Level	57
Cannon St to Dartford via Blackheath/Charlton	61
Charing Cross to Dartford via Blackheath/Charlton	60
Dorking North to Durnsford Rd depot empties	86 bar
Gillingham to Cannon St via Charlton/Blackheath	63
Hampton Court or Shepperton to Waterloo via East Putney special	86
Holborn Viaduct to Crystal Palace High Level	87
Maidstone West to Cannon St via Charlton/Blackheath	65
Nunhead and Crystal Palace High Level	2
Purley and Caterham	3
Victoria and Beckenham Jct via Streatham Hill and Crystal Palace	36
Victoria to Crystal Palace High Level	86
Waterloo and Wimbledon via East Putney	86
Wimbledon Park Sidings to Wimbledon Park empties	86 bar
Wimbledon Park Sidings to Wimbledon Park empties	none
Waterloo & Hampton Crt or Shepperton via East Putney empties	86 bar

P with bar above letter P̄

Cannon St to Gillingham via Blackheath/Chalton	63
Cannon St to Maidstone West via Blackheath/Charlton (to carry P dot between Gravesend and Maidstone W)	65
Charing Cross and Gillingham via Blackheath/Charlton	62
Charing Cross and Maidstone West via Blackheath/Charlton (to carry P dot between Gravesend and Maidstone West)	64
Dartford to Charing Cross via Charlton/Blackheath	60
Guildford and Aldershot	21
Holborn Viaduct to West Croydon via Herne Hill, Tulse Hill, Wimbledon, St Helier and Sutton	06

Purley and Tattenham Corner empties (race special)	02 bar
Victoria to West Croydon via Streatham Hill and Crystal Palace	06
Waterloo and Wimbledon Park via East Putney special	85

P with dot above letter Ṗ

Bromley North to Cannon St (not via Lewisham)	9
Gravesend to Maidstone West, det from Blackheath train	64, 65
London Bridge to London Bridge via Sydenham Crystal Palace and Tulse Hill	49
Purley and Tattenham Corner	2
Victoria and Crystal Palace Low Level empties	06 bar
Wimbledon to Blackfriars via Tulse Hill and Herne Hill	17

P with two dots above letter P̈

Blackfriars or Holborn Viaduct to Orpington via Nunhead, Lewisham and Beckenham Jct	85
Bromley North to Charing Cross (not via Lewisham)	10
Charing Cross or Cannon St to Bromley North (not Lewisham)	9, 10
London Bridge to London Bridge via Tulse Hill, Crystal Palace and Sydenham	94
Western section empties via East Putney	86 bar, 03 bar
Wimbledon Park to Wimbledon Park sidings empties	

S unmodified, ie no bar or dots above letter

Bickley to Blackfriars via Herne Hill	25
Cannon St and Dartford via Bexleyheath	71
Charing Cross to Dartford via Bexleyheath	70
Elmers End and Addiscombe	2
Gillingham to Cannon Street via Bexleyheath	73
Maidstone West to Cannon Street via Bexleyheath	75
Orpington to Blackfriars via Herne Hill	61

Victoria and Sutton via Streatham Common and West Croydon	30
Waterloo and Shepperton via Earlsfield	24

S with bar above letter S̄

Cannon St to Maidstone West via Bexleyheath (to carry S dot from Gravesend to Maidstone West)	75
Cannon Street to Gillingham via Bexleyheath	73
Charing Cross and Gillingham via Bexleyheath	72
Charing Cross and Maidstone West via Bexleyheath	74
Dartford to Charing Cross via Bexleyheath	70
Sevenoaks to Blackfriars via Orpington and Nunhead	63
Victoria and Selhurst via Streatham Common (empties to carry inverted V double dot)	32
Waterloo and Shepperton via Richmond	47

S with dot above letter Ṡ

Charing Cross or Cannon Street to Caterham	93
Gravesend to Maidstone West, on Bexleyheath line trains	74, 75
Tattenham Corner or Caterham to Cannon Street	93
Victoria to Epsom Downs via Streatham Common and West Croydon	84

S with two dots above letter S̈

Crystal Palace High Level to Blackfriars	57
Empties to Shepperton	24 bar from 1954
Gillingham or Fawkham to Blackfriars via Nunhead	93, later 39
Tattenham Corner or Caterham to Charing Cross	01
Victoria and Three Bridges via Redhill empties	56 bar
Wimbledon to Victoria via Streathm & Balham Jc empties	56 bar

T unmodified, ie with no bar or dots above letter

Cannon Street and Addiscombe via Lewisham	27

Charing Cross to Addiscombe via Lewisham	26
Horsham to East Croydon or Victoria via Three Bridges	48
Tattenham Corner and Selhurst	38
Waterloo and Portsmth Hbr via Earlsfield and Worplesdon semifast, not stopping at Havant	8
Waterloo and Windsor via Brentford	57
Waterloo and Woking via Earlsfield (until 1954)	10

T with bar above letter T̄

Addiscombe to Charing Cross via Lewisham	26
Cannon Street to Addiscombe via Ladywell Loop	37
Charing Cross to Addiscombe via Ladywell Loop	36
London Bridge to Holborn Viaduct via West Croydon and St Helier	21
Twickenham and Chertsey	14
Victoria and East Croydon via Strm Hill and Crystal Palace	8
Waterloo and Virginia Water via Weybridge	14
Waterloo and Windsor via Richmond	58
Weybridge to Chertsey or Virgina Water	14

T with dot above letter Ṫ

Addiscombe to Cannon Street via Ladywell Loop	37
Victoria (Eastern side) and Sutton via Herne Hill, Wimbledon and St Helier	08
Waterloo- Portsmth Harbour via Earlsfield and Worplesdon semifast, stopping at Havant	80

T with two dots above letter T̈

Addiscombe to Charing Cross via Ladywell Loop	36
Empty to work passenger Twickenham to Chertsey	14 bar
London Bridge to Tattenham Corner via Forest Hill	85

Portsmth Hbr to Woking (to couple to Alton train)	81
Virginia Water/Chertsey and Woking empties(until 1954)	13 bar
Waterloo and Portsmouth Harbour empties	8 bar
Waterloo and Woking via Earlsfield	10
Waterloo to Portsmth Hbr via Woking slow with rear to Alton	81

U unmodified, ie with no bar or dots above letter

Victoria and Epsom Downs via Selhurst empties	84
Blackfriars or Holborn Viaduct to Dartford via London Bridge and Sidcup	49
Dartford to Waterloo via Sidcup (special)	96
East Croydon to London Bridge via Selhurst, Tulse Hill (Xmas)	53
Elmers End and Sanderstead	3
Gillingham and Brighton via London Bridge (reverse) and Forest Hill	53
Gravesend to Holborn Viaduct via Sidcup and Nunhead	59
Plumstead to Peckham Rye to work U or 75 to Holborn Viaduct	75 bar
Waterloo to Twickenham via Teddington special	97
Western section special duties	various

U with bar above letter Ū

Brighton and Seaford special empties	28 bar
Eastbourne to Coulsdon North special	65
Gravesend or Dartford to Blackfriars or Holborn Viaduct via Sidcup and London Bridge	49
Holborn/Blackfriars to Gravesend via London Bridge and Sidcup	49
Twickenham to Waterloo via Teddington special	97
Victoria (Eastern) to Wimbledon South sidings via Herne Hill	79 bar
Western section specials	
Worcester Park to Portsmouth special empties	35 bar

U with dot above letter U̇

Blackfriars or Holborn Viaduct and Dartford via Nunhead and Sidcup	58
Gravesend to Blackfriars Or Holborn Viaduct via Sidcup and Nunhead	58
Streatham Hill to Littlehampton via West Croydon and Sutton special	73

U with two dots above letter Ü

Blackfriars or Holborn Viaduct to Gravesend via London Bridge and Sidcup	49
Blackfriars or Holborn Viaduct to Gravesend via Nunhead and Sidcup	89
Twickenham to Victoria via Wimbledon and Streatham special	56
Western section special empties	20 bar, 09 bar, etc
Wimbledon Park sidings to Wimbledon Park sidings via Teddington, Twickenham, Clapham Junction and reverse (to turn stock)	97

V unmodified, ie with no bar or dots above letter

Bickley to Victoria via Herne Hill	24
Blackfriars or Holborn Viaduct to Dartford via London Bridge and Greenwich	89
Cannon Street and Dartford via Greenwich	81
Cannon Street and Gillingham via Greenwich	83
Charing Cross to Dartford via Greenwich	80
Durnsford Road depot to Waterloo (passenger from Earlsfield)	61
Herne Hill and Victoria	74
London Bridge and Selhurst via Forest Hill	83
Maidstone West to Cannon Street via Greenwich	85
Sevenoaks to Victoria via Petts Wood and Herne Hill	70
Victoria-Guildford via Mitcham Junction and Epsom	02
Waterloo ML to Waterloo WL via Earlsfield, Teddington, Richmond	61

V with bar above letter V̄

Cannon St to Gravesend via Greenwich	85
Bickley to Victoria via Catford	26
Blackfriars or Holborn Viaduct to Gravesend via London Bridge and Greenwich	89
Charing Cross and Gravesend via Greenwich	84
Charing Cross and Gillingham via Greenwich	82
Dartford to Charing Cross via Greenwich	80
London Bridge and Selhurst via Tulse Hill	35
Maidstone West to Charing Cross or Cannon Street	84, 85
Sevenoaks to Victoria via Petts Wood and Nunhead	72
Streatham Hill and Bognor via Crystal Palace, West Croydon Sutton Horsham and Littlehampton (special)	29
Waterloo WL to Waterloo ML via Richmond Teddington and Earlsfield	62

V with dot above letter V̇

Down trains Gravesend to Maidstone West ex-Greenwich line	84, 85
London Bridge to London Bridge via Forest Hill, Selhurst and Tulse Hill	09

V with two dots above letter V̈

Waterloo to Strawberry Hill via Earlsfield empties	62 bar
Waterloo to Strawberry Hill via Richmond empties	62 bar
Waterloo to Teddington via Earlsfield empties	62 bar
Durnsford Rd depot to Teddington or Strawberry Hill empties	62 bar
Kingston or Shepperton to Strawberry Hill empties	62 bar
Blackfriars or Holborn Viaduct and Bromley North via London Bridge	48
Crystal Palace High Level to Victoria via Nunhead	86
Gravesend to Blackfriars or Holborn Viaduct via Greenwich and London Bridge	89

London Bridge to London Bridge via Tulse Hill, Selhurst and Forest Hill	90
Ascot and Woking empties	26 bar

d inverted P unmodified

Alton to Woking (if coupling to Portsmouth train)	7
Charing Cross and New Cross Gate empties	02 bar
East Croydon and Streatham Hill via Crystal Palace empties	20 bar
Portsmouth & Southsea to Waterloo slow (if coupling at Woking)	7
Victoria and New X Gate via Streatham Hill & Crystal Pal empties	51 bar
Waterloo to Portsmouth & Southsea via Earlsfield & Woking with rear to Alton detached at Woking (slow)	7
Western section empty trains to/from Durnsford Rd depot, inc various to/from Lancing works (Lancing number code was 04 bar)	various
Wimbledon Park sidings & Epsom Downs via Mitcham Jc (races)	08 bar
Woking to Portsmouth & Southsea slow (detached from Alton train)	7

d inverted P with bar above d̄

Waterloo and Portsmouth and Southsea via Earlsfield slow	57
Waterloo and Kingston via Richmond (from Sept 1958)	68
Western section empty trains (not after about 1950)	

d inverted P with dot above ḋ

Waterloo-Portsmth and Southsea via Earlsfield & Worplesdon fast, calling at Havant	70

d inverted P with two dots above d̈

Orpington or Swanley and Victoria via Beckenham Jc & Crystal Palace — bank holidays — empties	36
Waterloo and Portsmouth and Southsea via Earlsfield and Worplesdon semifast not calling at Havant	71
Western section empty trains (not after about 1950)	

Λ inverted V unmodified

Cannon Street and Sevenoaks via Petts Wood (not Lewisham)	17
Charing Cross to Sevenoaks via Petts Wood (not Lewisham)	16
East Croydon and Brighton via Redhill special	51
East Croydon and Brighton special	
Holborn Viaduct and Gillingham via Herne Hill	91
Kingston to Strawberry Hill	63
Victoria and Gillingham via Herne Hill	90
Victoria and Horsham via Mitcham Junc	86
Waterloo ML to Strawberry Hill via Earlsfield	63

Λ inverted V with bar above Λ̄

Waterloo WL to Strawberry Hill via Richmond	64
Sevenoaks to Charing Cross via Petts Wood (not Lewisham)	16
Holborn Viaduct and Fawkham via Catford	93
Victoria and London Bridge via Streatham Com & Norwood Jc (fish and parcels traffic in passenger trains)	7 bar

Λ inverted V with dot above Λ̇

London Bridge and Horsham via Forest Hill, West Croydon & Epsom	31
Sevenoaks to Cannon St via Petts Wood and Lewisham	19

Λ inverted V with two dots above Λ̈

Effingham Junction & Farnham via Guildford empties (from June 1954)	23 bar
Charing Cross and Sevenoaks via Lewisham and Petts Wood	18
Cannon St to Sevenoaks via Lewisham and Petts Wood	19
Victoria and Selhurst via Streatham Common empties	32 bar
Western section special empties	

Numeral headcodes for main line and 'second generation' suburban stock

(i) Central section headcodes — main line stock — passenger trains, 3 July 1939

	Between	and	via	train class
1	Brighton	West Worthing		
1	Preston Park	Brighton		
1	Horsted Keynes	Haywards Heath		
1	Lewes	Seaford		
1	Eastbourne	Ore		
1	Arundel	Littlehampton		
1	Bognor	Barnham		
2	Redhill	Reigate		
2	Horsted Keynes or Haywards Hth	Brighton		
2	Eastbourne	Polegate		
2	Three Bridges	Horsham		
3	London Bridge	Brighton	Quarry	fast
3	Arundel	Bognor	Littlehampton	
3	Arundel	Bognor	direct	
4	Victoria	Brighton	Quarry	fast
5	London Bridge	Brighton	Quarry	semi-fast
5	Three Bridges or Horsham	Littlehampton		
6	Victoria	Brighton	Quarry	semi-fast
6	Three Bridges or Horsham	Bognor	direct	
7	Three Bridges or Horsham	Bognor	Littlehampton	
7	London Bridge	Brighton	Quarry	slow
8	Victoria	Brighton	Quarry	slow
9	London Bridge	Brighton	Redhill	fast
10	Victoria	Brighton	Redhill	fast
12	Victoria	Brighton	Redhill	semi-fast
12	Bognor	Portsmouth Hrbr		
13	Littlehampton	Portsmouth (LL)		
14	Victoria	Brighton	Redhill	slow
15	London Bridge	Brighton	Redhill	slow
15	Chichester	Portsmouth (LL)		
16	Brighton	TO Ore	Eastbourne	
16	Victoria	Littlehampton	Quarry & Hove	
17	London Bridge	Littlehampton	Quarry & Hove	
17	Brighton	Lewes		
18	Ore	TO Brighton	Eastbourne	
18	Victoria	Littlehampton	Redhill & Hove	
19	London Bridge	Littlehampton	Redhill & Hove	
20	Victoria	Portsmouth Hbr	Mitcham Jc	
21	London Bridge	Portsmouth Hrbr	Mitcham Jc	
23	London Bridge	Portsmouth Hrbr	Quarry & Horsham	
24	Victoria	Brighton	Redhill	special
25	London Bridge	Portsmouth Hrbr	Redhill & Horsham	

	Between	and	via	train class
26	Victoria	Portsmouth Hrbr	Quarry & Horsham	
26	Brighton	Ore	direct	
27	London Bridge	Brighton	Quarry	special
28	Brighton	Seaford		
28	Victoria	Portsmouth Hrbr	Redhill & Horsham	
29	London Bridge	Brighton	Redhill	special
30	Brighton	Portsmouth Hrbr	Littlehampton	
31	Charing Cross	Reigate		
31	Brighton	Bognor	Littlehampton	
32	Brighton	West Worthing	Preston Park	
34	Victoria	Reigate		
35	Brighton	Littlehampton		
37	London Bridge	Portsmouth Hrbr	West Croydon & Guildford	excursion
37	London Bridge	Reigate		
37	Horsted Keynes or Haywards Hth	Seaford		
38	Streatham Hill	Brighton	Quarry	special
38	Tooting	Littlehampton	Wimbledon & Mitcham	excursion
39	London Bridge	Brighton	Streatham & Quarry	special
40	Victoria	Bognor	Mitcham Jc	
41	London Bridge	Bognor	Mitcham Jc	
42	Victoria	Brighton	Quarry	special
43	London Bridge	Bognor	Quarry & Horsham	
43	London Bridge	Bognor	Redhill & Horsham	
46	Victoria	Bognor	Quarry & Horsham	
46	Horsted Keynes or Haywards Hth	Lewes		
47	London Bridge	Bognor	West Croydon	
48	Victoria	Bognor	Redhill & Horsham	
49	Horsted Keynes or Haywards Hth	Eastbourne		
49	Tooting	Bognor	Wimbledon, Mitcham & Sutton (not Littlehmptn)	excursion

(Headcode H when run with suburban stock)

	Between	and	via	train class
50	Victoria	Littlehampton	Mitcham Jc	
51	London Bridge	Littlehampton	Mitcham Jc	
52	Victoria	Ore	Quarry & Eastbourne	
53	London Bridge	Littlehampton	Quarry & Eastbourne	
54	Victoria	Ore	Quarry & direct	
56	Victoria	Littlehampton	Quarry & Horsham	
57	London Bridge	Littlehampton	West Croydon, Horsham	
58	Victoria	Littlehampton	Redhill & Horsham	
59	London Bridge	Littlehampton	Redhill & Horsham	
60	Victoria	Ore	Redhill & direct	

Between	and	via	train class
60 Brighton	Portsmouth Hrbr		semi-fast
61 London Bridge	Ore	Redhill & Eastbourne	
62 Brighton	Portsmouth Hrbr		slow
62 Victoria	Eastbourne	Quarry	
63 London Bridge	Ore	Quarry & Eastbourne	
64 Victoria	Eastbourne	Redhill	
64 Brighton	Bognor	direct	
65 London Bridge	Eastbourne	Quarry	
67 London Bridge	Eastbourne	Redhill	
68 Victoria	Seaford	Quarry	
69 London Bridge	Seaford	Quarry	
70 Victoria	Portsmouth Hrbr	Mitcham Jc & Littlehampton	
71 London Bridge	Portsmouth Hrbr	Mitcham Jc & Littlehampton	
72 Victoria	Ore	Quarry & Redhill	
73 London Bridge	Portsmouth Hrbr	Quarry, Horsham & Littlehampton	
74 Victoria	Seaford	Quarry	
75 London Bridge	Portsmouth Hrbr	Redhill, Horsham & Littlehampton	
76 Victoria	Portsmouth Hrbr	Quarry, Horsham & Littlehampton	
78 Victoria	Portsmouth Hrbr	Redhill Horsham & Littlehampton	
79 London Bridge	Seaford	Redhill	
90 Victoria	Bognor	Mitcham Jc & Littlehampton	
91 London Bridge	Bognor	Mitcham Jc & Littlehampton	
92 Victoria	Bognor	West Croydon & Littlehampton	
93 London Bridge	Bognor	Quarry, Horsham & Littlehampton	
95 London Bridge	Bognor	Redhill, Horsham & Littlehampton	
96 Victoria	Bognor	Quarry, Horsham & Littlehampton	
96 Victoria	Bognor	Redhill, Horsham & Littlehampton	
02 Victoria	Gatwick, Plumpton, Lewes, Barnham or Chichester	Quarry	race special
03 London Bridge	as 02	Quarry	race special
04 Victoria	as 02	Redhill	race special
05 London Bridge	as 02	Redhill	race special
06 Brighton	Gatwick, Plumpton, Lewes, Barnham or Chichester		race special

The Quarry line route is the fast line avoiding Redhill.

(ii) Eastern section numeral headcodes — suburban and outer suburban, 1939-57

Between	and	via	train class
0 Elmers End	Hayes		
1 Strood	Maidstone West		
2 Elmers End	Addiscombe		
2 Nunhead	Crystal Palace HL		
3 Elmers End	Sanderstead		
8 London Bridge	Gillingham	Greenwich (to/from Brighton)	excn
9 Cannon Street	Bromley North	not via Lewisham	
10 Charing Cross	Bromley North	not via Lewisham	
12 Charing Cross	Orpington	not via Lewisham	
13 Cannon Street	Orpington	not via Lewisham	
14 Charing Cross	Orpington	Lewisham	
15 Cannon Street	Orpington	Lewisham	
14/15	to/from Sevenoaks from 1959		
16 Charing Cross	Sevenoaks	not via Lewisham	
17 Cannon Street	Sevenoaks	not via Lewisham	
17 Holborn Viaduct	to Sevenoaks	London Bridge (not Lewisham)	
18 Charing Cross	Sevenoaks	Lewisham	
19 Cannon Street	Sevenoaks	Lewisham	
20 Charing Cross	New Beckenham	Lewisham	
21 Cannon Street	New Beckenham	Lewisham	
23 Eastern section and Western section via Central section			special
23 Holborn Viaduct	Bickley	Herne Hill	
24 Victoria	Bickley	Herne Hill	
24 Charing Cross	Hayes	Lewisham	
25 Cannon Street	Hayes	Lewisham	
25 Blackfriars	Bickley	Herne Hill	
26 Victoria	Bickley	Catford	
26 Charing Cross	Addiscombe	Lewisham	
26 Charing Cross	Elmers End	Lewisham	
27 Cannon Street	Addiscombe	Lewisham	
27 Cannon Street	Elmers End	Lewisham	
27 Holborn Viaduct	Bickley	Catford	
28 Charing Cross	Selsdon or Sand'std	Lewisham	
29 Cannon Street	Selsdon or Sand'std	Lewisham	
29 Blackfriars	Bickley	Catford	
30 Charing Cross	New Beckenham	Ladywell loop	
31 Cannon Street	New Beckenham	Ladywell loop	
32 Herne Hill	Bromley South		
34 Charing Cross	Hayes	Ladywell loop	
35 Cannon Street	Hayes	Ladywell loop	
36 Charing Cross	Addiscombe	Ladywell loop	

	Between	and	via	train class
36	Charing Cross	Elmers End	Ladywell loop	
37	Cannon Street	Addiscombe	Ladywell loop	
37	Cannon Street	Elmers End	Ladywell loop	
38	Charing Cross	Selsdon or Sand'std	Ladywell loop	
39	Cannon Street	Selsdon or Sand'std	Ladywell loop	
40	Charing Cross	Sidcup or Dartford	not Lewisham	
41	Cannon Street	as 40	Parks Bridge	
42	Charing Cross	Gillingham	Parks Bridge	
43	Cannon Street	as 42	Parks Bridge	
45	Orpington	to Holborn Viaduct	London Bridge (up only)	
46	Charing Cross	Gravesend Central	Parks Bridge	
46	Charing Cross	Maidstone West	Parks Bridge	
47	Cannon Street	as 46	Parks Bridge	
48	Blackfriars or Holborn V	Bromley North	London Bridge	
49	Blackfriars or Holborn	Gravesend Central	London Bridge and as 46	
50	Charing Cross	Sidcup or Dartford	Lewisham	
51	Cannon Street	as 50	Lewisham	
52	Charing Cross	Gillingham	Lewisham	
53	Cannon Street	as 52	Lewisham	
53	Gillingham	Brighton	London Bridge	BH excn
56	Charing Cross	Gravesend Central	Lewisham	
56	Charing Cross	Maidstone West	Lewisham	
57	Blackfriars	Crystal Palace HL	Nunhead	
57	Cannon Street	Gravesend Central	as 50	
57	Cannon Street	Maidstone West	as 50	
58	Blackfriars or Holborn V	to Gravesend Central	Nunhead and Sidcup	
58	Gravesend Ctl	to Blackfriars (not Holborn)	Sidcup and Nunhead	
59	Blackfriars or Holborn V	to Gravesend Central	London B and as 58	
59	Dartford	to Holborn Viaduct	Sidcup and Nunhead	
60	Charing Cross	Dartford or short thereof	Blackheath Charlton	
61	Cannon Street	Dartford or short thereof	Blackheath Charlton	
61	Blackfriars	Sevenoaks	Herne Hill & Orpington	
62	Charing Cross	Gillingham	Blackheath Charlton	
63	Cannon Street	Gillingham	Blackheath Charlton	
63	Blackfriars	Sevenoaks	Catford & Orpington	
64	Charing Cross	Gravesend C or Maidstone W	Blackheath Charlton	
65	Cannon Street	Gravesend C or Maidstone W	Blackheath Charlton	
65	Blackfriars	Sevenoaks	Herne Hill & Swanley	
67	Blackfriars	Sevenoaks	Catford & Swanley	

	Between	and	via	train class
68	Blackfriars or Holborn V	Gravesend Central	Nunhead, Charlton	
69	Blackfriars or Holborn V	Gravesend Central	London B and as 64	
70	Charing Cross	Dartford	Bexleyheath	
70	Victoria	Sevenoaks	Herne Hill & Orpington	
71	Cannon Street	Dartford	Bexleyheath	
71	Holborn Viaduct	Sevenoaks	Herne Hill & Orpington	
72	Charing Cross	Gillingham	Bexleyheath	
72	Victoria	Sevenoaks	Catford loop & Orpington	
73	Cannon Street	Gillingham	Bexleyheath	
73	Holborn Viaduct	Sevenoaks	Catford loop & Orpington	
74	Charing Cross	Gravesend C or Maidstone W	Bexleyheath	
74	Victoria	Herne Hill		
75	Cannon Street	Gravesend C or Maidstone W	Bexleyheath	
75	Holborn V or Blackfriars	Herne Hill		
76	Blackfriars or Holborn V	Cannon Street		
76	London Br Low Level	Gravesend Central	Bexleyheath	
76	Holborn Viaduct	Sevenoaks	Chislehurst Swanley	
78	Blackfriars or Holborn V	Gravesend Central	Nunhead, Bexleyheath	
79	Blackfriars or Holborn V	to Gravesend Central	London B, Bexleyheath	
79	Gravesend or Dartfd	to Holborn V (not Blackfr)	Bexleyheath, Nunhead	
80	Charing Cross	Dartford or short thereof	Greenwich	
80	Victoria	Sevenoaks or short	Herne Hill and Swanley	
81	Cannon Street	Dartford or short thereof	Greenwich	
81	Holborn Viaduct	Sevenoaks or short	Herne Hill and Swanley	
82	Charing Cross	Gillingham	Greenwich	
82	Victoria	Sevenoaks	Catford and Swanley	
83	Cannon Street	Gillingham	Greenwich	
83	Holborn Viaduct	Sevenoaks	Catford and Swanley	
84	Charing Cross	Gravesend C or Maidstone W	Greenwich	
85	Cannon Street	Gravesend C or Maidstone W	Greenwich	
85	Blackfriars or Holborn Vdt	Orpington	Nunhead, Lewisham, mid-Kent, Bickley	
86	Victoria	Crystal Palace HL	Nunhead	
87	Holborn Viaduct	Crystal Palace HL	Nunhead	
89	Blackfriars or Holborn V	Gravesend Central	London B & Greenwich	
90	Victoria	Gillingham	Herne Hill	
90	Gillingham	to Waterloo East	Dartford & North Kent	special

Between	and	via	train class
01 Holborn Viaduct	Gillingham	Herne Hill	
02 Victoria	Gillingham	Catford loop	
03 Holborn Viaduct	Gillingham	Catford loop	
03 Charing Cross	to Caterham		
03 Cannon Street	to Caterham		
03 Tattenham/Caterham	to Cannon Street		
04 Victoria	Maidstone East	Herne Hill	
04 Sanderst'd or Hayes	Waterloo	Lewisham	special
05 Holborn Viaduct	Maidstone East	Herne Hill	
06 Victoria	Maidstone East	Catford loop	
07 Holborn Viaduct	Maidstone East	Catford loop	
07 Charing Cross	Reigate	Redhill	
01 Maidstone East	Beckenham Jc	special	
02 Victoria	Streatham Hill	Herne Hill	empties
02 Charing Cross or Cannon Street	New Cross Gate		empties
03 Holborn Viaduct	Streatham Hill	Herne Hill	empties
04 Ramblers excursions			special
05 Cannon Street	Sevenoaks	Chislehurst, Swanley	
06 Charing Cross	Sevenoaks	Chislehurst, Swanley	
07 Cannon Street	Gillingham	Chislehurst, Swanley	
08 Charing Cross	Gillingham	Chislehurst, Swanley	
09 Cannon Street	Maidstone East	Chislehurst, Swanley	

(no Charing Cross equivalent of 09)

(iii) Empty electric main line stock trains in suburban area — from 3.7.39

Between	and	via
1 London Bridge	Streatham Hill	Tulse Hill
01 London Bridge	Selhurst	Forest Hill
02 Victoria (Eastern section)	Streatham Hill	Herne Hill & Tulse Hill
03 Holborn Viaduct	Streatham Hill	Herne Hill & Tulse Hill
05 London Bridge	Streatham Hill	Forest Hill & Crystal Palace
06 London Bridge or Peckham Rye	to Victoria	Denmark Hill
07 London Bridge	Selhurst	Tulse Hill
08 Victoria	Selhurst	Norbury
09 London Bridge	to Victoria	Forest Hill & Norbury
30 Victoria	Guildford	Mitcham Jc & Epsom
Victoria	Streatham Hill	
London Bridge	New Cross Gate	
London Bridge	Peckham Rye	
32 Streatham Hill	Maidstone East	Crystal Palace
38 Cannon St or Holborn	Grove Park	Nunhead
54 Cannon St	Durnsford Rd	Blackfriars

(iv) Western section — main line stock — passenger headcodes from 3.3.39

Between	and	via	train class
2 Waterloo	Portsmouth Hrbr	Chertsey	
3 Waterloo	Portsmouth & S'sea	Epsom	
4 Waterloo	Portsmouth Hrbr	Epsom	
5 Waterloo	Portsmouth & S'sea	Cobham	
6 Waterloo	Portsmouth Hrbr	Cobham	
7 Waterloo	Portsmouth & S'sea	Earlsfield & Woking	
8 or 80 Waterloo	Portsmouth Hrbr (headcode 80 if calling at Havant)	Earlsfield & Woking	
9 Waterloo	Portsmouth & S'sea	Chertsey	
10 Waterloo	Woking	Earlsfield	
12 Waterloo	Alton (up trains coupling at Woking to carry headcode 7)	Earlsfield	
13 Waterloo	Woking	Chertsey	
14 Waterloo	Virginia Water	Earlsfield	
15 Waterloo	Alton	Chertsey	
15 Waterloo	Effingham Jc	Epsom	
16 Waterloo	Guildford	Epsom	
17 Waterloo	Dorking or Horsham	Epsom	
17 Waterloo	Windsor	Brentford	
17 Staines	Weybridge	det from or att to train via Brentford	
18 Waterloo	Windsor	Richmond	
18 Staines	Weybridge	det from or att to train via Richmond	
18 Waterloo	Chessington South		
19 Waterloo	Worcester Park, Epsom or Leatherhead		
20 Waterloo	Ascot	Earlsfield & Woking	
20 Guildford	Alton		
21 Guildford	Aldershot		
24 Waterloo	Shepperton	Wimbledon	
25 Waterloo	Woking	Brentford & Ascot	
26 Waterloo	Woking	Richmond & Ascot	
27 Waterloo	Reading	Brentford	
28 Waterloo	Reading	Richmond	
30 Waterloo	Hampton Court		
37 Waterloo	Alton	Brentford & Ascot	
38 Waterloo	Alton	Richmond & Ascot	
42 Waterloo	Guildford	Cobham	
43 Waterloo	Effingham Jc	Cobham	
47 Waterloo	Shepperton	Richmond	

	Between	and	via	train class
61	Waterloo (ML)	Waterloo (WL)	Wimbledon, Teddington and Richmond	
62	Waterloo (WL)	Waterloo (ML)	Richmond, Teddington and Wimbledon	
85	Waterloo	Wimbledon Park	special	
86	Dorking line	Waterloo	East Putney (special)	
86	Hampton Court	Waterloo	East Putney (special)	
86	Shepperton	Waterloo	East Putney (special)	
87	Waterloo	Wimbledon	East Putney	
87	Waterloo	Waterloo	Richmond, Hounslow and Brentford	
89	Waterloo	Waterloo	Brentford Hounslow and Richmond	
03	Windsor	Portsmouth Southsea	Woking	(special)
04	Windsor	Portsmouth Harbour	Woking	(special)

	Between	and	via	train class
05	Waterloo	Portsmouth Southsea	East Putney	(special)
06	Waterloo	Portsmouth Harbour	East Putney	(special)
07	Waterloo	Portsmouth Southsea	Woking	(special)
08	Windsor	Portsmouth Harbour	Woking	(special)
09	Windsor	Ascot	Chertsey	(special)

(v) Western section — empty trains — main line stock

7	Waterloo	Fratton	
12	Alton	to Durnsford Rd depot	Earlsfield
15	Farnham	to Chertsey	
68	Durnsford Road	Waterloo	

Other empty journeys of main line stock carried appropriate passenger code with bar over.

Above:
For the London-Brighton and Worthing express services, 23 six-car units, each with a Pullman car, were constructed, numbered 2001-20 and 2041-3. Nos 2001-20 seated 72 first and 236 third; Nos 2041-43 seated 138 first and 120 third. All were classified '6COR' until the Eastbourne pantry units were built in 1935; Nos 2001-20 then became '6PUL' and 2041-3 became '6CIT'. Nos 2041-3 had a high proportion of first class accomodation and mainly worked on the 'City Limited' (Brighton and London Bridge) business train, at 8.45am from Brighton and 5.00pm from London Bridge. All were renumbered, to 3001 etc, in January 1937.

This view shows unit No 2019 with Pullman car *Peggy*, standing in Gatwick sidings when new. *Ian Allan Library*

Right:
Pullman first class interior, probably original, date unknown *Ian Allan Library*

Left:
One of the most famous trains in the world: the 'Brighton Belle'. Three five-car all-Pullman electric units were built; as Nos 2051-53 they commenced service on 1 January 1933 as the 'Southern Belle' Pullman train. On 29 June 1934 the train was renamed 'Brighton Belle'. They were given their more familiar unit numbers 3051-53 in January 1937. Pullmans were withdrawn during the war years, but the 'Belle' returned in May 1946; it finally bowed out on Sunday 30 April 1972. This view shows an unidentified unit on trial south of Three Bridges. *Ian Allan Library/C. E. Brown*

Left:
Down 'Belle' near Merstham on the Quarry Line.
Ian Allan Library/D. Sellman

Below left:
Down 'Belle' passing Tooting Bec box; note
semaphore signals. *G. Waterer Collection*

Above:
A down Victoria-Littlehampton train with 6PUL
No 3005 passes the old Gatwick Airport station.
G. Waterer Collection

Below:
6CIT No 3043 with Pullman car *Ruth* at London
Bridge on 9 April 1949 on the 1.5pm Saturday only
to Brighton. *G. Waterer Collection*

Above:
The next major extension of electrification came on 7 July 1935, from Haywards Heath to Lewes, Eastbourne and Ore (a hamlet beyond Hastings, included because the depot was built there), Brighton to Seaford, and Haywards Heath to Horsted Keynes.

The 6PAN units comprised two motor third brake saloons, two trailer thirds, a trailer first and a first class trailer with a pantry — a small kitchen which could serve tea, boiled eggs and toast but little else. It was their limited scope which caused the pantries to be abandoned, locked out of use from sometime in the 1950s.

With the Eastbourne scheme came the 2BIL, with motor third brake and driving trailer composite, both with side corridor and a lavatory but without a gangway connection. The electrical equipment was suburban and the BIL could work with suburban, 2NOL and 4LAV stock. The first 10 were numbered 1890-9 until 1937 and then became Nos 2010-1/09 in the unit renumbering scheme. Further batches were built for the Portsmouth No 1 scheme (1937), Portsmouth No 2 (1938) and the extension from Staines to Reading and Aldershot (1939). In 1935, 17 six-car pantry units commenced work with the Eastbourne, Hastings and Seaford electrification. These were units Nos 2021-37, renumbered to 3021-37 in January 1937. No 2036 is seen here on a trial run early in 1935 near Pevensey Bay.
Ian Allan Library

Above right:
6PAN No 3022 enters Eastbourne with an SR Mogul in the background, on 11 July 1959.
Ian Allan Library/N. Caplan

Right:
6PAN No 3023 waits for departure from London Bridge to Brighton. *G. Waterer Collection*

Above:

The Portsmouth No 1 scheme, to Portsmouth and Alton via Woking, was to be next after Eastbourne. Work commenced in October 1935, a few months after the Eastbourne opening, and full electric services between Weybridge and Virginia Water started on 3 January 1937. Newly converted 2NOL units Nos 1863-82 had already come to the Western section, and these and Nos 1883-90 were allocated to the services via Staines, displacing three-car suburban units.

Trials between Waterloo and Portsmouth Harbour, and between Woking and Alton, started in April 1937. For the fast Portsmouths, of which there were four an hour each way on Saturdays during the holiday season, 48 four-car corridor units with gangways throughout — the first Southern units so fitted, were built. Twenty-nine, Nos 3101-29, were designated 4COR, with two motor third brakes, a trailer third and a trailer composite. To work with them — normally in the centre of a 12-car train — were 19 4RES units, Nos 3054-72, having two motor third brakes, a third class kitchen/dining car, and a first class diner with compartments and a small saloon. All coaches were built by the SR at Eastleigh works except the kitchen and diner first cars, which came from Metropolitan Cammell and Birmingham Railway Carriage & Wagon Co respectively. The Portsmouth express stock also worked Monday — Friday rush hour trains to Farnham and Alton. The Portsmouth No 1 allocation of 2BIL units for stopping services was 38, numbered 2011-48. The scheme also allowed for

some extra suburban work, for which the last three-car suburban units, Nos 1579-84, were converted from L&SWR steam stock.

The Portsmouth No 2 scheme dealt with the mid-Sussex line from Three Bridges through Horsham to Portsmouth, and the coast line from West Worthing to Littlehampton, Bognor Regis and Havant. A new fast service linked Victoria and Bognor/Portsmouth, dividing at Barnham. The stock comprised another 26 4COR units, Nos 3130-55, working with a new concept — the 4BUF, units Nos 3073-85. The 4BUF had the usual two motor third brakes, but marshalled between them were a trailer composite and a buffet car. The 4BUF unit worked the Bognor portion of the train. Along the coast, the Victoria-West Worthing 6PUL formations worked through to Littlehampton; PULs also worked to Eastbourne, and Eastbourne PAN units ran to Littlehampton.

For the Portsmouth No 2 local services, 68 2BIL units, Nos 2049-2116, were built. BIL construction continued to 2152, to provide the 36 units neeed for the Reading electrification which was opened on 1 January 1939.

For the Portsmouth electrification, the express formation and front end design were radically changed, and the result was 4RES, 4COR and 4BUF. Here new unit No 3056, destined to be formed as a RES with kitchen and dining cars but running as a non-restaurant 4COR formation, is near Buriton, between Rowlands Castle and Petersfield on a Portsmouth Harbour to Waterloo train before the introduction of the full electric service on 4 July 1937. Photo taken 6 May 1937. *Ian Allan Library*

Left:
4COR No 3120, taken in May 1938, probably at Fratton depot. This may have been the authorised route to Eastleigh works to have the second set of electrical jumpers inserted on the right-hand side (as seen: ie, cab left) which would have made for more convenient coupling arrangements when working the Victoria-Bognor/Portsmouth services which would commence in July 1938.
Ian Allan Library/ B. Q. Butt

Above:
The 10.30am Portsmouth Harbour to Waterloo approaches Woking Junction on 16 September 1946.
Ian Allan Library

Right:
Arriving at Portsmouth Harbour, a special excursion, probably from Barnes, headed by 4COR No 3111. *G. Waterer*

Below right:
COR units sometimes appeared on suburban duties. Here 4COR No 3144 heads the 5.15pm Waterloo-Horsley via Epsom, passing Queen's Road Battersea (now Queenstown Road) on 2 September 1955. The odd twist to this is that the 5.15pm, although a suburban service, was normally rostered as an 8BIL. No 3144 was one of the units with larger-than-standard unit numbers. *L. A. Mack*

Below:
Passing Havant, a Saturday-only Portsmouth-Waterloo nonstop, with No 3116 leading.
Ian Allan Library/ C. P. Brook

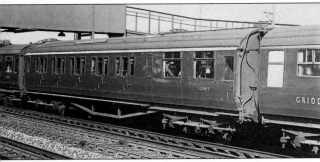

Above:
4COR No 3116 heads the 12.50 Waterloo-Portsmouth Harbour through Vauxhall on 11 October 1961. *Ian Allan Library*

Left:
At Havant, a rare close-up view of a restaurant first, No 12240 of 4RES No 3068, showing its five single compartments and tabled saloon, separated by a toilet.
Ian Allan Library

Left:
Corridor composite No 11812 of 4COR No 3122, also at Havant.
Ian Allan Library

Left:
The interior of a 4RES kitchen car, when new in June 1937. *Ian Allan Library*

Below:
First class compartment of a 4COR unit, new in March 1937. *Ian Allan Library*

Right:
1938 saw 13 of the buffet car variant of the Portsmouth stock; here, 4BUF No 3083 is arriving at Arundel on the 5.4pm Victoria to Littlehampton.
Ian Allan Library/P. J. Sharpe

Below right:
The 2BIL units, built for main line local and branch services, were well liked and comfortable. They had a side corridor, a toilet in both coaches, and were widely used used on the Western and Central sections.
No 2017 is on an up Portsmouth and Alton stopping service at Woking. *G. Waterer Collection*

Left:
The Brighton and West Worthing local service was worked with 2NOLs until 1957, when BILs and HALs took. 2BIL No 2078 pauses at Aldrington Halt.
Ian Allan Library

Right:
2BILs were the mainstay of the Brighton-Portsmouth semifast and stopping services: No 2037 calls at Angmering. *Ian Allan Library*

Below right:
Longhampton: not a new station, not closed and forgotten, but Christ's Hospital renamed for making the film 'Rotten to the Core'. 2BIL No 2150 heads the 10.36 Victoria to Boignor Regis on 13 March 1965.
Ian Allan Library/J. Scrace

Below:
Ford station on 2 May 1967. 2BIL No 2125 waits for the Littlehampton connection. The black triangle on the yellow warning panel was for platform staff and gave advance warning that there was 'No brake van at the other end of this unit' — avoiding confusion about where to try to load luggage and parcels.
Ian Allan Library/J. A. M. Vaughan

Top:
The 6pm Gravesend Central to London Bridge via the North Kent line was a regular 4SUB working; it ran on empty to Blackfriars where this train is arriving. On this occasion, in June 1958, a HAL formation, headed by No 2617, has been used.
G. Waterer

Above:
Medway HAL units, and the subsequent Western section batch Nos 2677-92, could often be found on the Central section, especially after 1958 when about 30 were transferred to work the Victoria-Gatwick Airport-Littlehampton service. Here, No 2637 leads a Brighton to West Worthing train, probably in 1959. *Ian Allan Library*

Brighton-Portsmouth trains crossing at Ford on
2 May 1967. The 'down' (westbound) train includes
2BIL No 2150, and the 'up', 2HAL No 2616.
Ian Allan Library

Above:
Four BILs, a NOL and a South London unit were
lost by war damage, and a NOL was written off after
an accident. After the war they were replaced by
seven steel-bodied Hals, Nos 2693-9. Here one of
the replacements, No 2699 with a 's' prefix to the
unit number and highlighted lettering is seen leaving
Victoria on the 12.28pm to Maidstone East via the
Catford loop, on 2 April 1949. *G. Waterer Collection*

Above:
In the late 1930s the Southern began design work on a general purpose electric locomotive. Three were ordered before the outbreak of World War 2. For goods haulage they were provided with a booster unit in the form of a flywheel driven generator which supplied power to the traction motors whilst the loco traversed gaps in the conductor rail. The Co-Co result, numbered CC1, appeared in 1941, and CC2 in 1943. They were used on freight trains between Norwood Yard and Chichester or Polegate, and after the war, on Newhaven boat trains. No CC1 is seen here in original condition on a test run on 24 January 1942. Electric mu-type headcode panel and plates were provided and used, although locomotive lamp brackets were also fitted. *Ian Allan Library*

Above right:
Under the BR numbering scheme, CC1 became 20001. The front end was altered and the headcode panel was replaced by fixed lamps and discs; in turn these were replaced by a roller blind headcode box. *Ian Allan Library*

Right:
No CC2, seen here at Barnham with British Railways lettering and with multiple-unit jumpers added. In 1948 CC2 was selected for a livery experiment; it was repainted light blue/grey with silver lining along the top and bottom of the body sides, and silver lettering shaded black; bogies and underframe were black. *Ian Allan Library/L. Elsay*

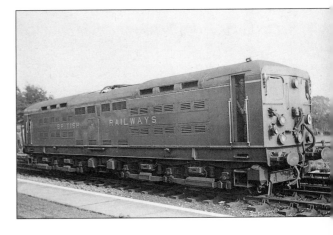

Top:
No 20002, formerly CC2, seen at Eastleigh loco works open day on 5 August 1964, with just a roller blind indicator, and two-tone horns fitted in place of the original chime whistle. *G. Waterer*

Above:
No 20003, the third of the SR's Co-Cos, was a more powerful machine and the front end design was modified, matching the contemporary 4SUB front. It was delivered in 1948 in SR malachite green with yellow lining and 'British Railways' applied in old gold Gill Sans. The whistle placed high on the cab roof. Here it on 2 March 1950 at Brighton on a Birkenhead-Hastings Saturday extra. *Ian Allan Library*

Above:
No 20003, in showroom condition, in black livery on exhibition at Waterloo on 22 March 1950. *Ian Allan Library*

Below:
The first of 24 electric locomotives built for the Kent coast electrification, No E5000 is shown here at Stewarts Lane depot in malachite green, with pale grey cab window surrounds, and a red and white lining band along the body side. Four lamp brackets were fitted to the front end, the upper two for normal train headboards. The headcode panel has the original Southern Region style of roller blind, with large figures; this was later replaced by smaller blinds which included letters as well as numbers, the letters being intended use on freight trains. *G. Waterer*

Top:
Until the arrival of Nos E5000-24, the Southern's electric loco fleet of two went almost unnoticed. A Bo-Bo shunter numbered 74S in the SR departmental series was built by the L&SWR in 1900 for the Waterloo & City line; from 1915 it spent its life above ground at Durnsford Road, shunting wagons on the power station coal ramp until it was scrapped in the early 1970s. *Ian Allan Library*

Above:
Rather older, smaller and certainly far less seen was No 75S, a four-wheeler which was technically Ao+A, built by Siemens in 1898. It spent its whole life in the Waterloo & City line depot, only emerging to be preserved at the National Railway Museum in York *G. Waterer*

Above:
In 1940 the original Waterloo & City stock was replaced by new cars built by English Electric. One every 10 years or so they would be taken to Lancing for overhaul. Here, three cars of the stock are at Wimbledon, waiting to be returned to Waterloo via East Putney, around 1960. *G. Waterer*

Below:
Photographed here at Waterloo north sidings, now swept away for the Eurostar platforms, W&C motor coach No 61 is at the head of the train. This coach is now at York Museum awaiting preservation. *G. Waterer*

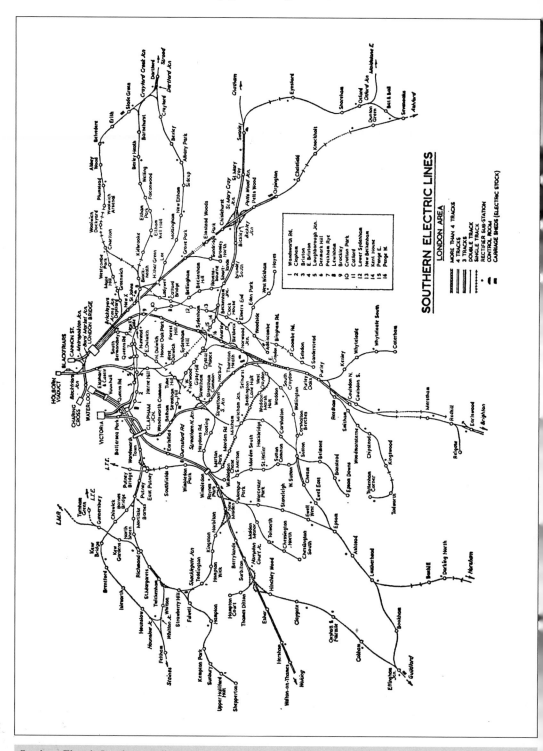

Southern Electric London area lines

Overnight Berthing Allocations of Electric Stock to Depots and Stations, Summer 1955.

1. Central Section

	2NOL	2BIL	4LAV	4SUB	6PUL	6PAN	5BEL	4COR	4BUF	4EPB	2EPB
Barnham								1			
Bognor Regis		9						7	5		
Brighton	7	10	3	1	2						
Caterham										4	
Coulsdon North				16							
Crystal Palace				11							
Dorking North				10							
Eastbourne	6	3				2					
Epsom				6							
Epsom Downs				10							
Haywards Heath	4										
Horsham		5	2	4							
Leatherhead				3							
Littlehampton		5			4			2	2		
London Bridge			2	10							
Lovers Walk	3	12	8	1	4	5		1			
New Cross Gate			2	12							
Ore	5		2		6						
Peckham Rye											2
Preston Park					3	3					
Reigate		6	1								
Seaford	4					2					
Selhurst				21							5
Streatham Hill				7				3	1		
Tattenham Corner										8	3
Three Bridges		4	1								
Victoria			5	3			2				
Wallington				6							
West Croydon				10							
West Worthing	4	1	1			2		1			
Wimbledon South				12							1
Total Central	33	55	27	143	19	14	2	15	8	12	11

2. Eastern Section

	2HAL	4SUB	4EPB	2EPB	4DD
Addiscombe		11	4		
Beckenham JC		7			
Bickley		6			
Blackfriars		6			
Bromley North		3	2	1	
Cannon Street		2	4	1	
Charing Cross		9			
Dartford			12	4	
Gillingham	22	6	6		
Gravesend Central			2		
Hayes		3			
Herne Hill		2			
Herne Hill SS South		5			
Maidstone Barracks	11				
Maidstone East	6				
Orpington		23	5	1	
Plumstead		6			
St Mary Cray		2			
Sevenoaks		7	1		
Slade Green	2	7	26	2	2
Streatham Hill (E/sectn)	11				
Swanley	3	6			
Victoria	4				
Total Eastern	59	102	71	9	2

3. Western section

	2NOL	2BIL	4SUB	4COR	4RES	4EPB
Aldershot		5				
Ascot		3				
Chertsey	7	2				2
Effingham Jc		8				8
Farnham		8		10	4	
Fratton		2		9	3	
Guildford		8				2
Hampton Court		8				
Hounslow		10				
Portsmouth Harbour		8	1	6	3	
Portsm & S'sea		8				
Portsm Dn Carr Sdgs		6		2	1	
Reading South		6				
Shepperton		6				
Strawberry Hill		17				4
Waterloo	8	8	9			2
Wimbl'n Pk Sdgs & Durnsford Rd	4	32	14	5	1	10
Windsor & Eton R	12					
Woking		9				
Total Western	31	103	75	32	12	28

Totals, all SR

	2NOL	2BIL	2HAL	4LAV	4SUB	6PUL	6PAN	5BEL	4COR	4RES	4BUF
All sections	64	158**	59**	27	320	19	14	2	47	12	8
Engineering spares	12	**	**	8	***	1	3	1	11	4	5
Fleet totals	76	148	99	35	***	20	17	3	58	16	13

** Bil fleet 148 — 127 working, 21 spare; HAL fleet 99 — 59 working, 8 spare on Eastern section , 32 HAL units covering balance of Bil workings and engineering spares.
***SUB and 4EPB fleet total about 500; engineering spares about 70

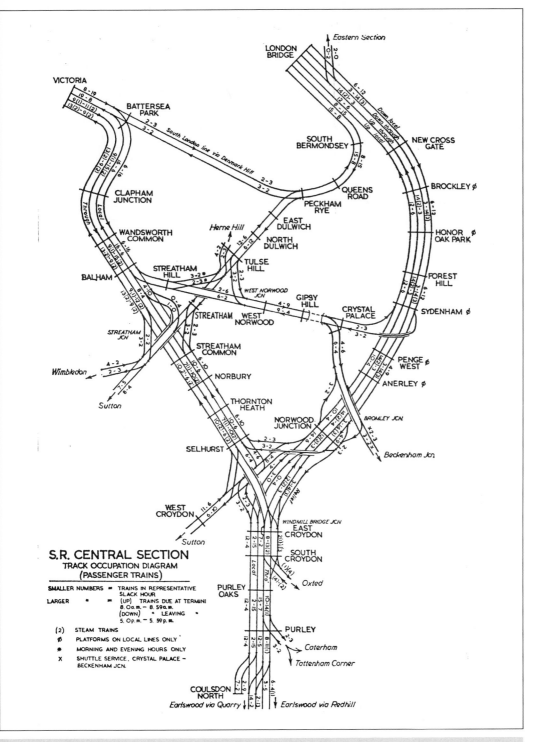

SR Central Section track occupancy diagram, 1959.

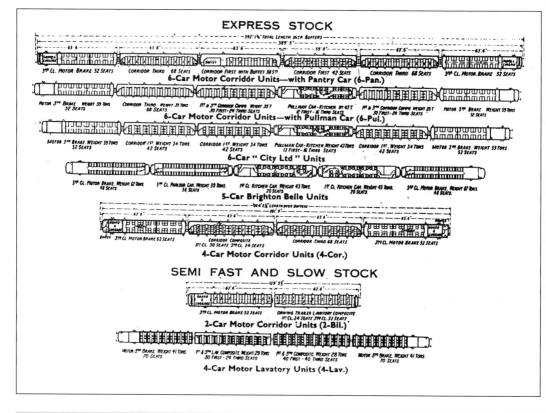

EXPRESS STOCK

6-Car Motor Corridor Units—with Pantry Car (6-Pan.)

6-Car Motor Corridor Units—with Pullman Car (6-Pul.)

6-Car "City Ltd" Units

5-Car Brighton Belle Units

4-Car Motor Corridor Units (4-Cor.)

SEMI FAST AND SLOW STOCK

2-Car Motor Corridor Units (2-Bil.)

4-Car Motor Lavatory Units (4-Lav.)

Above:
Typical Southern Electric rolling stock, 1943.

Above right:
The steel-bodied 4SUB stock, which occupied numbers 4101-30, 4277-99, 4355-87, 4601-07 and 4621-754 in the unit list, totalled 227 units. All of them were built at Eastleigh works, most of them on underframes salvaged and reconditioned from conversions of the 1925-38 period. No 4101, the first unit in the plan, had been due in the autumn of 1939 and was completed about September 1941.
Nos 4102-10 followed in 1944-5. These coaches, although steel sided, had wooden roofs. In an effort to deal with rising traffic, these units seated 468 passengers which was the highest seating capacity on the Southern and far more than any previous design: too many, in fact. A rethink by the Southern Railway in 1945 resulted in larger compartments, fewer seats, and for good measure a completely restyled front end which appeared in 1946 and which set the visual standard on the Southern for the next 35 years.
    Units 4111 onwards had all-steel body shells. Nos 4121-30 were an experiment with saloons of three or four bays, with off-set centre gangway but retaining separate doors for each bay of seats.
Nos 4355-78 continued the all-compartment arrangement, but Nos 4378-87, 4277-99 and most subsequent units had three saloons and one compart-ment coach. Nos 4601-7 (second series) were 'odd' in having two compartment trailers. The compartment trailers in these and in Nos 4667-754 came from augmented units which were becoming life-expired. In 1939 designs were drawn up for a new generation of suburban unit to replace the ex-steam conversions of 1914-38. Most were to be on existing underframes, but the programme was to start with 10 all-new units, which were to introduce the term '4SUB' to a whole generation of railway enthusiasts. The war delayed production but Nos 4101-10 were all complete by April 1945. Very clean No 4103 is seen here arriving at Purley Oaks on a down Victoria-Coulsdon North service. *Ian Allan Library*

Right:
One of the first 10 units, nicknamed 'Shebas' ('a very great train'), No 4105, is leading on a Sevenoaks to Holborn Viaduct service, passing the old signalbox at Shortlands. *Ian Allan Library/ R. C. Riley*

Right:
4SUB No 4114 passes Mitcham Junction heading towards Sutton. *Ian Allan Library*

Centre right above:
4SUB No 4129 lettered 'Southern' on the front, at London Bridge on an up Gillingham to Cannon Street service; the platformless middle loop, between the old Platforms 4 and 6, was still in use. *G. Waterer*

Centre right below:
At Epsom, 4SUB No 4627 on an up Horsham to London Bridge duty. The internal layout of these units, with three saloon coaches and one compartment trailer, was standardised for new or rebuilt Southern suburban units from 1949 onwards. *Graham Waterer*

Below:
Unit No 4683 on the Sundays-only 9.42am Waterloo to Horsham, at Wimblehurst Road, Horsham, on 10 May 1959. This series of 4SUB units had the so-called 'Eastern section' motor bogie, originally fitted to conversions *c*1925-6; it had a longer wheelbase than the SR standard type. *Ian Allan Library/J. Scrace*

Above right:
In 1949 the Southern, concerned at the worsening
overcrowding on the Eastern section suburban
services to Dartford, produced a radical
experiment in the shape of two double-deck units,
Nos 4001-2. Each unit seated 552, giving 1,102 for
an eight-car train compared with 772 in the last
variation of the 4SUB series. The first of them,
No 4001, is seen on a test run on 14 September
1949 on the Brighton main line south of Haywards
Heath. *Ian Allan Library*

Right:
At Charing Cross before it was buried beneath an
office block, No 4002 is ready for its inaugural run
to Dartford via Bexleyheath on 1 November 1949.
The letters 'SR' on the old station roof were taken
down when Charing Cross was rebuilt and
reinstated on the new structure. *Ian Allan Library*

Below right:
Side view of the double-decker at Charing Cross.
The downfall of these units was the time taken in
loading and unloading; they also cost over 50%
more to build than the contemporary SUB/EPB
design, which used existing underframes and
bogies, so instead, the Southern opted for 10-car
trains of orthodox design, which began to run in
1955. *Ian Allan Library*

Below:
Despite its drawbacks, the double-decker was kept
in service; here it is on 12 June 1959, leaving
Cannon Street with the City of London in the
background. *Ian Allan Library*

Right:
The Southern Region had experimented with electro-pneumatic braking and a lighter, more efficient traction motor. Eastleigh's suburban design was modified to incorporate these plus unit-to-unit buckeye couplers, motor generators for lighting and control current, and a roller blind headcode display, and the draughty external cab doors were done away. The result was the 4EPB; the first unit, No 5001, was completed at the end of 1951, and production was almost continuous until 1957. Like the later 4SUBs, three coaches were saloons and had new all-steel body shells on reconditioned underframes, and the fourth was a compartment trailer of 1946-9 vintage from an augmented unit. These units were numbered 5001-53 and 5101-260. Most of them seated 386, all third class (which became second class before the series was complete). This is the cab interior of an early example. *Ian Allan Library*

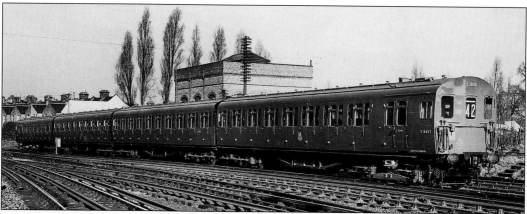

Above:
No 5001, the first of the 4EPBs, is shown here at Wimbledon Park sidings on 1 November 1951. The motor coach is numbered 8657, following on from the last of the SUB units; it was renumbered into a new series, as 14001, before it entered service. *Ian Allan Library*

Right:
4EPB No 5151 at Waterloo about to depart for Guildford on 1 March 1955. *L. A. Mack*

84

Top:
Unit No 5020, departing Waterloo East *c*1959, showing rear blinds turned to white blank, and carrying a tail lamp. Eventually, headcode blinds incorporated a red exposure which rendered the oil-powered tail lamp redundant. *Ian Allan Library*

Above:
Down Charing Cross to Hayes train, passing under the Catford Loop line bridge near Catford Bridge, with unit No 5179. *Ian Allan Library/J. Scrace*

Above:
Unit No 5039 arrives at London Bridge on a Charing Cross to Sevenoaks service.
Ian Allan Library

Right:
As the Southern Region's largest class, after the augmented SUBs had been withdrawn, 4EPBs were everywhere in the suburbs. Here No 5030 is berthed in the down siding at Hounslow with a 4SUB in the background.
Ian Allan Library/ R. E. Vincent

Right:
Unit No 5247 leads a London Bridge to Tattenham Corner train passing Norwood Junction.
Ian Allan Library

Top:
London Bridge as it was before the platforms were
extended to accommodate 12-car suburban trains; the
work was completed just as traffic fell in the early
1990s, and 12-car suburban trains have never yet run
in passenger service. In this view, No 5194 is on the
right leaving for Gravesend; in the centre another
4EPB is bound for Sevenoaks. *Ian Allan Library*

Above:
St Johns on 19 July 1958. Much has changed since.
The near siding and the main line platform were
removed in the 1970s, tracks were realigned and a
reversible loop was put in where the sidings had
been. The local line platform has been extended to
take 12-car trains. *Ian Allan Library/B. Oliver*

Above:
The development of British Rail's standard carriage designs caught up with the Southern electric system in 1954, starting with the 2EPB suburban unit, followed by a main line local services version, the 2HAP, with some first class compartments and a lavatory; and then by the 4CEP. The 4CEP was the logical development of the 4COR, and was designed for the Kent coast electrifications of 1959-62. Buffet-car units, designated 4BEP, were built to run with the 4CEPs on domestic fast services to Ramsgate and Dover, and on the Folkestone Harbour and Dover Harbour boat trains. There was also a BR standard version of the 4EPB, with minor differences in internal layout, and 'SR' versions of the 2EPB and 2HAP using reconditioned underframes. Construction of this stock occupied Eastleigh carriage works until 1962.

Unit numbers for these types are listed elsewhere in these pages; in the 1980s, some stock, particularly HAP units, was withdrawn as surplus to requirements or beyond economic refurbishment. Of units which survived, some units were reformed, and many, including most of the CEPs, were rebuilt or at least altered internally; in the process, all the survivors were renumbered.

The Southern's first BR standard electric units, designated 2EPB, were built to replace the 2SL and 2WIM units on the South London and Wimbledon-West Croydon lines, and for the introduction of 10-car trains on the South Eastern lines. The first 2EPB, No 5701, works the 12.17 Victoria to London Bridge at Battersea Park in the snow on 2 March 1954. *Ian Allan Library/N. W. Spinks*

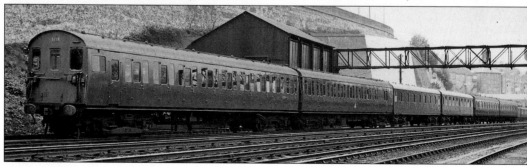

Left:
A 2EPB on a Sanderstead to Elmers End train leaving Selsdon. The line between Woodside and Selsdon was closed in October 1980. Part of it will live again in Tramlink.
Ian Allan Library/L. Sadler

Left:
A main line version of the 2EPB, the 2HAP, followed the 2EPB. No 6005 is seen when new at Eastleigh works; 173 of these units were constructed between 1958 and 1963.
Ian Allan Library

Below left:
A view of Peckham Rye depot, now demolished and replaced by a small housing estate. It was constructed by the LB&SCR for the South London line electrification. The shed in the distance was used as a lifting shop for SR main line 6PUL, 6PAN, 4COR/RES/BUF units. 2EPB No 5708 passes on a Victoria to London Bridge service.
Ian Allan Library/R. C. Riley

Bottom left:
2EPB units Nos 5717/18 with two trailer coaches from Hastings diesel unit No 1007 during test runs between London and Brighton, photographed at Lovers Walk, Brighton on 7 May 1957. The reason for the tests is now lost in the mists of time.
Ian Allan Library/M. W. Jackson

Above right:
2HAP No 6014 working a Maidstone West to Strood service at Aylesford in 1958. *Ian Allan Library*

Centre right:
Also at London Bridge in the early 1960s, a Charing Cross to Maidstone West train leaves Platform 2 headed by 2HAP No 6025; the original blinds have been replaced by the smaller numeral variety in a masked panel. *Ian Allan Library/P. J. Sharpe*

Right: On the middle siding at Sheerness-on-Sea is 2HAP No 6055. *G. Waterer*

Above:
Two HAP units at Sittingbourne, No 6076 nearest the camera, waiting to work the shuttle to Sheerness. *Ian Allan Library/P. J. Sharpe*

Right:
The HAP units worked throughout Kent. Two units leave Canterbury East on a Sheerness-Dover Priory service; a Class 33 diesel electric loco is in the goods yard. *Ian Allan Library*

Below right:
The 2NOL units converted in the late 1930s had become life expired by 1957 and two-car versions of the 4EPB, with reconditioned underframes and bogies, replaced them. The first 36, designated 2HAP, were designed to 'Southern' technical specifications; they included first class compartments and a lavatory. Here, unit No 5612, incorrectly numbered 5012, is at Eastleigh carriage works Open Day in August 1958. *G. Waterer*

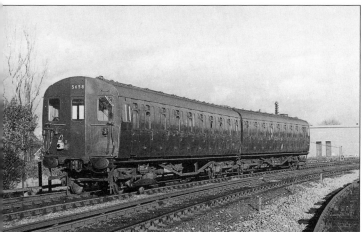

Above:
'SR' HAP No 5604, showing the corridor side of the driving trailer composite, at Ramsgate on 1 June 1959, two weeks before full electric services began over the Gillingham-Ramsgate route.
Ian Allan Library/ J. C. Haydon

Left:
The suburban version of the 'SR' two-car unit, designated 2EPB and numbered 5651-84, spent much of its working life on the Waterloo, Weybridge and Windsor services.
No 5658 is seen leaving Staines for Windsor; at this time tail end blinds were still white and a tail lamp had to be carried.
Ian Allan Library/J. C. Beckett

Left:
Two of the 'SR' 2EPB units at Virginia Water, No 5660 leading.
Ian Allan Library/P. J. Sharpe

Above:
Two 2EPBs depart Staines for Windsor around 1960; the down goods yard is still open and clearly very well used.
Ian Allan Library/P. J. Sharpe

Right:
4CEP No 7103 leading a 12-car train which formed the 08.52 (SX) East Croydon to Victoria on 14 June 1956. The substation in the background and the covered walkway to the old St John's Hill station entrance have now gone, and the Granada cinema has closed. *L. A. Mack*

Right:
For a short while in 1958-9 before they were needed for the Kent coast electrification, CEP units worked on the Central Division. No 7126 is at Clapham Junction on an up train from Portsmouth Harbour. *G. Waterer*

Above:
Another Central Divsion view: No 7123 on a test run at Wallington. *G. Waterer*

Left:
Canterbury West station in July 1959, with Southern Railway luggage trolley, 1950s canopy lamp shades, and No 7146 working the 12.36pm Sheerness to Dover Priory. *G. Waterer*

Below left:
Motor luggage vans were built to work in multiple with CEP/BEP units betwen Victoria and the channel ports, Dover and Folkestone. They were fitted with battery traction so as to be able to work on the quay sides where the third rail could not be installed. They could also haul parcels or freight vans if required. No 68001 is photographed at Stewarts Lane depot. *G.Waterer*

Above:
Rush hour at Charing Cross with all six platforms full with EPB stock, *c*1960.
Ian Allan Library/R. C. Riley

Right:
Slade Green Depot as it was in the mid-1950s; it was converted from a steam shed in 1926. Two trains of EPB stock are berthed, and between one of the rare 'roller blind' 4SUB units.
Ian Allen/R. C. Riley

Right:
The power station at Durnsford Road; in the background is the L&SWR electric shed built in 1914. Electric shunting loco No 74S is at the bottom of the coal ramp. Passing is the 'Bournemouth Belle' with 'Merchant Navy' class No 35014 *Netherland Line*.
Ian Allan Library/R. C. Riley

Above:
An unusual scene: 6PAN unit 3021 heads the 9.18am Victoria to Bognor Regis out of Horsham. It was rare for six-car units to get on to the mid-Sussex line. This view was taken on Sunday 10 October 1965. No 3021 still had a few months to go before withdrawal, and thus far had escaped the yellow warning panels which began to appear on front ends in November 1963.
Ian Allan LibraryJ. Scrace

Above left:
At Epsom station with the old signalbox aloft, with 4SUB No 4627.
Ian Allan Library/P. Sharpe

Left:
Over the years the Southern had added halts to its network; one such was Southease and Rodmell, a remote spot on the Seaford branch. 2BIL unit No 2027 is on a Seaford-Horstead Keynes service on 26 April 1959. *Ian Allan Library*

Above:
Wimbledon flyover on 20 November 1951; an up suburban train formed of an 'original' L&SWR unit climbs the Durnsford Road flyover, while a late 1940s steel-bodied 4SUB passes on a down Kingston roundabout train. In the distance Durnsford Road power station is steaming hard to generate the current for these and other trains.
Ian Allan Library

Centre right:
How many enthusiasts who were around in the 1950s and 1960s like to remember the Southern electric system for the unfussy comfort of the BIL units? Here two of them depart from Virginia Water on an up Reading/Guildford service.
Ian Allan Library

Right:
Another nostalgic scene: a train of 4COR units passes Vauxhall in 1966 on a down Portsmouth semi-fast service. The photogrpaher's vantage point was Coronation Buildings, one of several tenement blocks erected by the L&SWR to accommodate families displaced by the widening of the line out of Waterloo during the early 1900s. The tall chimney on the right marked the United Dairy bottling plant for which a train of milk tankers occupied Platform 1 at Vauxhall every morning after the rush hour until lunchtime. The milk was piped from platform level, down and under the station and the main road outside. *Ian Allan Library*